Pearson
PUBLISHING

Student Handbook for Religious Education

Dr Mike Kirby
with Phil Emmett

Consultant editors: Val Emmett and Simon Hughes

Illustrations by Julie Beer, Nic Brennan and Virginia Gray

Photographs supplied by Phil and Val Emmett: Pictures of Religion

Name ....

Class ....

School ....

Dates of exams ....

Exam board ....

Specification number ....

Candidate number ....

Centre number ....

Further copies of this publication may be obtained from:

Pearson Publishing
Chesterton Mill, French's Road, Cambridge CB4 3NP
Tel 01223 350555   Fax 01223 356484

Email info@pearson.co.uk   Web site www.pearsonpublishing.co.uk

ISBN: 1 85749 842 4

Published by Pearson Publishing 2003
© Pearson Publishing 2003

First published 1999
Second edition 2003

Contents

Introduction

This handbook has been written for students learning about Religious Education in secondary schools. It provides a comprehensive background to the world's major religions.

Aimed at students at Key Stages 3 and 4, the handbook has many possible uses including as a course book, homework aid, reference source or revision guide. A-level students and teachers new to RE will also find it useful as a reference source.

Christianity receives the fullest treatment in this book reflecting the reality that most examination specifications followed by students in the UK have at least one Christianity option. Christianity remains the main source religion used in RE as required by law.

Using this book

Remember that this is your book, so you may decide to personalise it, make notes in the margin, add to the glossary, etc. Questions are included at the end of each chapter to test your knowledge and understanding.

The glossary at the back of the book will help you to learn the meanings of new words. To make things clearer, most spellings are taken from the *Religious Education Glossary of Terms* (SCAA, 1994) unless religions are known to prefer otherwise.

RE code is used for references to things like the Bible. All of them follow the normal pattern for RE and are there to help you find sources of information. For example, Mt = The Gospel of St Matthew; Mk = The Gospel of St Mark; and so on. Note the following:

- Any quotations from the Hebrew Scriptures, the Old Testament or the New Testament are taken from the New International Version of the Bible.
- Out of respect for Jewish beliefs we have used 'G-d' in *Chapter 3*.
- BC and AD have been used in Christianity. BCE and CE are used elsewhere.

1 Christianity

✝ Essential Facts

Origins | The land now called Israel in the first century AD

Present spread | Throughout the world

Founder/prophets | Jesus Christ

Major beliefs | The Trinity (God in Three Persons); Jesus as 'the word of God'; Jesus' resurrection from the dead; sin, judgement and salvation; the kingdom of God

Sacred writings | The Holy Bible

Special places of worship | Churches, chapels

Special times | Advent, Christmas, Lent, Good Friday, Easter Day, Pentecost

Religious leaders | Bishops, priests, ministers, deacons, elders, pastors

Places of pilgrimage | Jerusalem, Lourdes, Walsingham (Norfolk), Vatican City, St Peter's in Rome and great cathedrals (eg Canterbury)

Holy day | Sunday

Forms of worship | Prayer, praise, Holy Communion, Ministry of the Word (preaching/teaching), good works

Groups | Roman Catholic, Eastern Orthodox Churches, Reformed Churches (Protestant)

✝ Jesus and the Gospels

What is Christianity?

Christianity is the religion founded on belief in the life and teachings of Jesus Christ, a Jew who lived about 2000 years ago in the land that is now Israel. It takes its name from Christ and its beliefs are practised in a variety of ways by about 950 million followers. Christianity is the largest of all world religions.

The cross, signifying the death of Jesus on behalf of mankind, came to be used by Christians as a symbol of the meeting place between man and God

What are the Gospels?

The **Gospels** are written accounts of what Jesus did, taught and achieved. They are the most important source in the study of Christianity. From the Gospels Christians obtain much of their knowledge and understanding of Jesus. There are four Gospels – those written by Mark, Matthew, Luke and John – and they are included in the **New Testament** section of the Bible.

Gospel means 'good news'. The writers intended to proclaim the good news that Jesus was the Son of God and that his death and **resurrection** had brought **salvation** to the world.

What do the Gospels say about Jesus?

Although Jesus was born a human being, the Gospels describe his birth as miraculous. Christians believe that he was not conceived by human sexual intercourse, but by the power of God. This is known as the 'Virgin Birth'.

The Gospels say that when Jesus was about 30, he was baptised by an influential preacher named John the Baptist. This event marks the start of Jesus' ministry, a period of about three years during which he travelled widely through Palestine (Israel):

- preaching about the Kingdom of God (see page 6)
- teaching people how to live in order to reach heaven
- healing those who were sick and infirm.

Palestine at the time was controlled by the Romans. Many Jews wanted to be free from Roman rule and hoped that God would send his **Messiah** (saviour) one day to lead them to victory over their enemies. Once news of Jesus' teachings spread, people began to talk about him as the possible Messiah. However, Jesus made it clear that his mission was not to defeat the Romans. Rather, he wanted to help people by saving them from **sin** and to put them in the right relationship with God.

By the standards of the time, what Jesus had to say on religious questions was radical. He often clashed with the Jewish religious authorities. Eventually, he was arrested by the Jewish leaders and tried on a charge of blasphemy, because it was said he had claimed to be the Son of God. A death sentence was passed which was subsequently endorsed by the Roman Civil Authority who saw him as dangerous.

The central belief of Christianity is that Jesus was crucified and then 'rose from the dead' (resurrected). Having come back to life, he reappeared to his disciples on a number of occasions.

What did Jesus teach?

Jesus calls Peter to be a disciple

- Jesus called people to enter 'the Kingdom of God', to accept God's rule and to live as God expected them to (see Mk 4 26-32).
- He taught that God is a God of love and like a loving parent. He tried to stop people being afraid of God (see Lk 15 11-32).
- He stressed that God is willing to forgive people who disobey Him providing they have a change of heart (repent) and seek His blessing (see Lk 19:1-10).
- Jesus used parables (stories about everyday life with a meaning) to teach how his own suffering and death was an opportunity for people to reject sin and return to a true relationship with God (see Jn 6:52-59).
- Jesus healed the sick to show that he had the power to forgive sins.

Why do Christians think Jesus is important?

Belief in Jesus is central to being a Christian. There are four main reasons why Christians think Jesus is important:

- Christians believe that Jesus is the **risen Lord**. The end of his life on Earth was not the end of his existence. He ascended into heaven and remains alive with God. This gives Christians hope that there is a life after death for them, too (see 1 Cor 15:42-50).
- Christians believe that Jesus is the **Son of God**. In Jesus God became human (see Acts 2:36).
- He was someone who **unveiled** the truth. Christians think that through the example of his own life he showed people what God was like: a compassionate, forgiving God who showed concern for humanity.
- Christians see Jesus as a **teacher**. He has shown them a way of life and given them a set of values. Central to his teaching are the beliefs that God is like a loving parent and that everyone should treat each other well: *'Love the Lord your God with all your heart... and your neighbour as yourself'* (Mt 22:37).

What do Christians mean by 'God'?

Christians believe that there is one God, the Creator and ruler of the universe; He is infinite (without limit) and eternal (without beginning or end). God is also believed to be all-powerful (omnipotent) and all knowing (omniscient). Yet Christians emphasise that He is not impersonal or remote. They believe that God can be approached personally.

What is the Trinity?

Christians believe that there is one God in three persons, 'Father, Son and Holy Spirit'. This is the **Trinity** (from tri-unity, 'three-in-one'). These three elements, or existences, live in each other and each represents God in a particular form:

- **God the Father** is the Creator, the power behind the world.
- **The Son of God** is one of the titles given to Jesus who Christians believe is the **incarnation**, or human form, of God.
- **The Holy Spirit** is the continuing presence of God in the world. The Holy Spirit works through people and situations to encourage the qualities of love and freedom from sin which were seen in Jesus himself.

This belief in God as the Trinity is unique to Christianity.

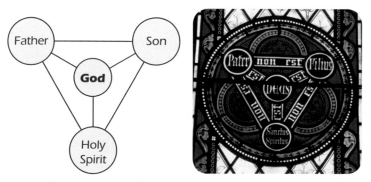

The concept of the Trinity depicted in a stained glass window

What is the Kingdom of God?

Christians believe that Jesus' life on Earth had a purpose which was to announce the good news that the Kingdom of God ('rule of God') had arrived. The Kingdom seems to refer to a spiritual experience that believers share, and which affects all aspects of their individual and communal life. The Gospels say that believers share in the Kingdom now by turning away from sin and following the teachings of Jesus. However, the Kingdom will not be complete until some time in the future.

> 'Take heed, watch and pray; for you do not know when the time will come.' (Mk 13:33)

What is the 'Second Coming'?

Many Christians believe that when the Kingdom on Earth is complete, this will coincide with Jesus' return – the Second Coming. Some Christians say that Jesus will return in a form that everyone will see. Other Christians think that Christ will return as a spiritual influence that will inspire the whole of humanity.

What is sin?

Christians believe that people are blessed by God with a feeling for what is right. Sin means to go against this feeling wilfully and therefore to disobey God. The Bible warns that all people are sinners and therefore face judgement.

What is salvation?

Salvation is the idea that God is prepared to forgive people their sins. This was made possible by the death and resurrection of Jesus. Christians believe that sinners can still be united with God in heaven as long as they repent and follow the example of Jesus. To repent means to feel sorrow for the wrong done and to seek forgiveness through turning to God, and being open to the teachings of Christ. The Christian message warns that if a person fails to seek forgiveness for their sins they will not be at peace with themselves, others or God.

Christians believe in the idea of hell as the ultimate punishment for a person who continues to disobey God.

Jesus the Lamb of God who was sacrificed to save people

In the same way that no one can accurately describe heaven, Christians have relied on differing symbols or images to describe hell. The main concept to grasp is that it is the place where God is not.

What is the Christian view of heaven and hell?

Many Christians believe in the idea of judgement in the afterlife where people will be called to account for their sins. Those who have repented and followed Jesus' teachings, enter heaven. Those who have shut Christ out of their life go to hell.

All those who have died and entered heaven are often referred to by Christians as the Communion of Saints (see Mt 25:31-46).

However, the Christian view of heaven and hell has been interpreted in different ways down the ages. Modern interpretations are divided between those who emphasise the love and forgiveness of God and hold that no one is finally damned, and those who stress that the wicked will be eternally punished.

Christian worship includes teaching about what Jesus said and did

✞ Sources of Authority

Why is the Bible important in Christianity?

Christianity has one Bible which is divided into two major parts, known as the **Old Testament** and the New Testament. The Old Testament contains 39 books of Jewish scripture, while the New Testament features 27 books of Christian scripture. There are an additional six books, known as the **Apocrypha**, that Roman Catholics regard as scripture.

Christians believe that the Old Testament and the New Testament describe how God reveals Himself, how He acts and why He acts in this way. The two testaments together are known as the 'Word of God' since they progressively develop Christian understanding of God.

Indeed many New Testament events are predicted in the Old Testament. Jesus said:

> *'Think not that I have come to abolish the law and the prophets; I have come not to abolish them but to fulfil them.'*   (Mt 5:17)

Christians believe that the Biblical texts were inspired and directed by God. However, they do not revere the Bible as a physical object. This is because Christians want to remember that it is the living Jesus who is important, not information about Him.

What are the Creeds?

Over time the Christian Church has drawn up lists of its most important beliefs. These are called **creeds**, from the Latin word *credo*, meaning 'I believe'. There are three great creeds of the Church:

- **The Apostles' Creed** – Dates from the fourth century AD. It was not actually written by the 12 **apostles**, but it was based on their teaching:

I believe in God, the Father almighty,
creator of heaven and earth.

I believe in Jesus Christ, his only Son, our Lord.
He was conceived by the power of the Holy Spirit
and born of the Virgin Mary.
He suffered under Pontius Pilate, was crucified, died and
was buried.
He descended to the dead.
On the third day he rose again.
He ascended into heaven,
and is seated at the right hand of the Father.
He will come again to judge the living and the dead.

I believe in the Holy Spirit,
the holy catholic Church,
the communion of saints,
the forgiveness of sins,
the resurrection of the body,
and the life everlasting. Amen.

- **The Nicene Creed** – Resulted from a meeting of Church leaders in 325 AD known as the Council of Nicaea. A modified form is used in Church service books today. This is the most important creed in the **Orthodox** tradition.

- **The Athanasian Creed** – Was based on the teachings of a Christian theologian Athanasius, who lived in the fourth century AD.

Creeds are used in many forms of Christian worship, such as **baptism**, **confirmation** and the **Eucharist** (see page 15).

Orthodox church

✝ The Christian Church

What is the Church?

Christians often view the Church as a community of people who share the same religious beliefs and may meet together to worship. The Church is also described as the 'body of Christ'. This means that the Church has the responsibility of representing Christ on Earth.

What was the early Church like?

The early Christians spread the message of Jesus so that by the end of the first century there were many Christians throughout Asia Minor, Greece and Rome. This was the beginnings of the early Church. For the next two centuries, the Church experienced persecution from the Roman authorities. In the fourth century, however, the Roman Emperor Constantine converted to Christianity and the persecutions stopped.

In 313 AD, Christianity was made the official religion of the Roman Empire, with its centre in Rome. The Bishop of Rome, known as *il papa* (the **Pope**), became the supreme leader of the Church on Earth.

St Peter's, Rome

Why did divisions occur in the Church?

The early Popes dreamt of a worldwide Church, representing all nations and bringing peace to the world. After a while, however, various groups started separating from the main Church. A breach developed between the Western Latin Church and the Eastern Greek Church. In the eleventh century they finally split into two churches, the **Roman Catholic** and the **Orthodox**. The main reasons for this division were:

1 Differences of opinion about how **liturgy** (worship) should be conducted.
2 The specialness of icons – paintings or images which were a focus for worship in the Eastern Church.
3 The addition to the creed by the Western Church, of a clause which suggests that the Holy Spirit comes from Jesus as well as God.

Another major division occurred in the sixteenth century. This came about as a result of advances in printing and translation. This allowed ordinary people to read the Bible for themselves. A movement known as the Reformation questioned many of the traditional teachings and would no longer accept the Pope as leader. The new churches which were set up by the 'reformers' or 'protestors' were called **Protestant**. The Protestant reformers soon split into a number of rival groups. The Church of England also broke away from Rome for political reasons at the time of the Reformation, but it kept many of the traditional beliefs.

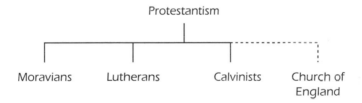

Protestantism

Moravians   Lutherans   Calvinists   Church of England

What are the main branches of the Church today?

The main Christian churches or 'denominations' today are:

- **The Roman Catholic Church** has the Pope as leader. About half the Christians in the world are Roman Catholics. They believe that St Peter was the first Bishop of Rome and carried on the work of Christ. Each Pope in turn has handed on the truths given by Christ in person to Peter.

A Roman Catholic church in Sri Lanka

- **The Orthodox Churches** are found mainly in Eastern Europe but with branches in Western Europe and the USA. They follow a traditional pattern of worship that, in many ways, has changed little since the time of the early Church. Orthodox Churches are groupings of Churches in different areas. Some have patriarchs over them and some have archbishops. Some patriarchs are given more honour than others, such as the Patriarch of Constantinople, who is known as the Ecumenical Patriarch.

- **The Anglican Church** is made up of Churches in various countries worldwide. It includes the Church of England, which was created in 1534 AD when King Henry VIII ruled that the Pope had no authority in the English church. The Anglican Church has combined traditions from the older Roman Catholic Church with some Protestant ideas. All Anglican Churches have the Archbishop of Canterbury as their main leader.

- **The Free Churches** (**non-conformists**) are distinguished mainly by the fact that they reject the authority of the Pope and bishops. They differ from the Church of England in rejecting the idea that the church and state should be linked.

This beautiful church 'in the round' is in Denmark

What is ecumenism?

Ecumenism is the idea that Christians should come closer to each other by, for example, taking part in services and group meetings. It is the product of the desire of local Christians to come together despite differences to work as one 'body of Christ'.

In modern times, the ecumenical movement has been led by the World Council of Churches which was founded in 1948 AD to cope with the problems faced by competing missionaries. The Council is a union of Protestant churches engaged in extending Christian unity throughout the world.

✝ Christian Worship

Where do Christians worship?

Christians worship in private as well as in groups. Christians meet for worship in churches, chapels or in small groups in other places. 'Church' in this sense means both a community of worshippers and the building where worship takes place. The 'church' as a building is designed so that every aspect of it focuses attention on the purpose of worship.

What is the purpose of worship?

Most Christians believe that the Church as a community of worshippers is 'the body of Christ'; in other words, it is the sign of Christ's continuing presence in the world. Christians seek to maintain this link with Christ through worship and in the way they live.

What are the main features of Christian worship?

There are many different types of worship within Christianity. Every denomination has its own form of worship and even between churches of the same denomination there may be differences. However, general features of Christian worship include:

- Sunday is observed as a holy day.
- Worship is offered to God through Jesus His Son. This is because Christians believe that they come to know God through Jesus.
- The idea that when Christians meet together to offer reverence and praise this represents an act of worship on behalf of all people.
- Ministry of the Word, where Christians hear readings from the Bible, usually including one from the Gospels. There is a sermon (teaching) about the meaning for Christians today.
- Study of the Bible by individuals and small groups.
- Prayer and praise (eg the singing of **psalms** and other hymns).
- Many Christians participate in the Eucharist (see page 15) as their main form of worship.

Why do Christians pray?

Prayer is a common feature of worship among Christians. In some traditions prayer follows a set pattern or form of words; in others, there are no set rules and the practice of prayer is characterised by considerable variety.

Roman Catholics praying at a church in Colombo, Sri Lanka

Through prayer Christians seek to experience God for themselves. Prayer usually takes one of the following forms:

* Praising God's greatness.
* Thanksgiving for God's goodness and providence (looking after human needs).
* Requesting God's forgiveness, or other acts of blessing.
* Approaching God on behalf of others (intercession).

Jesus gave a model of prayer which Christians call the Lord's Prayer:

> *'This, then, is how you should pray:*
> *Our Father in heaven,*
> *hallowed be your name,*
> *your kingdom come,*
> *your will be done*
> *   on earth as it is in heaven.*
> *Give us today our daily bread.*
> *Forgive us our debts,*
> *   as we also have forgiven our debtors.*
> *And lead us not into temptation,*
> *   but deliver us from the evil one.'*   (Mt 6:9-13)

Why are there different styles of church building?

The different styles of church building reflect the different styles of worship. For example, in an Anglican church the **altar** is the focus of the building. It is set apart to create a feeling of mystery and awe.

By comparison, the furnishings in a non-conformist church are usually less ornate. This reflects the fact that generally less emphasis is given to ritual and symbolism in the act of worship, and more to the spoken word.

Anglican church

Non-conformist church

What is the Eucharist?

This is the most important act of worship for most Christians. It is also known as **Mass**, **Holy Communion** and the **Lord's Supper**. The Eucharist celebrates the Last Supper of Jesus and his disciples.

Bread and wine are used in the service to represent the body and blood of Christ. By drinking the wine and eating the bread, Christians focus their attention on the great act of sacrifice made by Jesus and his gift of salvation. By participating in the Eucharist, Christians express their belief that they can be saved from sin or separation from God through the suffering of Christ.

For churches of the Orthodox and Roman Catholic traditions, the Eucharist or Mass is the main service, often held daily. This is because they believe that Jesus is really present in the bread and wine.

A stained glass window depicting the Last Supper

For other Christian denominations, it may be celebrated less frequently, usually fortnightly or monthly, because the service is commemorating Jesus' very special actions at the Last Supper.

The Eucharist is an example of a special kind of worship, known as a **sacrament**, in which taking part is a sign that the worshipper receives God's love or **grace**. The Roman Catholic and Orthodox churches recognise seven sacraments: Baptism, Confirmation, Holy Orders, The Eucharist, **Penance** (or **confession**), Sacrament of the Sick and Marriage.

Most Protestant denominations accept only two sacraments – Baptism and the Eucharist, because these are the only ones that Jesus is reported as being involved in himself in the Gospels.

Why is baptism important for Christians?

Jesus was baptised by John the Baptist at the beginning of his ministry. This showed that he was fully dedicating himself to God's work. Christians believe that they should do the same.

Most Christians believe that baptism recognises the entry of Christ into a person's life. Traditionally, the person to be baptised is immersed in water as a symbol of death and burial, and then brought out of the water and clothed in white, to be welcomed into the Christian Church as a sign of the new life.

Today, some churches baptise infants because Jesus said:

> '*Let the children come to me; do not try to stop them; for the kingdom of Heaven belongs to such as these.*'
> (Mt 19:4)

However, some Christians are critical of infant baptisms, arguing that it is meaningless to the baby. Believer's baptism is an alternative to infant baptism. The person to be baptised must be old enough to understand the meaning of the ceremony and to express their faith in Christ.

Baptism by total immersion

✠ Special Times and Pilgrimage

What are the special times for Christians?

Special times for Christians are closely connected with the life of Jesus:

- **Advent** begins the Christian year. It celebrates the coming of Jesus. It is also a time for remembering His promise that He will come again in glory to judge the world.
- **Christmas** marks the day of Jesus' birth and is celebrated on 25 December by Protestants and Roman Catholics, and on 9 January by the Orthodox Church. Christians thank God for the gift of His Son at Christmas. They celebrate by exchanging presents.
- **Lent** is a period of reflection and repentence leading up to Easter. It starts on **Ash Wednesday** and continues for 40 days.
- **Holy Week** is the period of seven days before Easter. It starts with Palm Sunday and includes Maundy Thursday, **Good Friday** and Holy Saturday (see page 18).
- **Easter Day** celebrates the resurrection of Jesus.
- **Ascension** is celebrated 40 days after Easter, commemorating Jesus being taken into heaven.
- **Pentecost** (Whitsun) celebrates the occasion when the Holy Spirit came among the apostles and the Christian Church was born.

What are the most important times in Christianity?

Easter is the most important time for Christians because it celebrates the resurrection and the promise of eternal life.

To prepare for Easter, there is a 40-day period called Lent. It recalls the time Jesus spent in the wilderness thinking about the work ahead (see Lk 4:1-13). It begins on Ash Wednesday when there may be a ceremony in which the forehead is marked with ashes. This is a reminder to reflect on whether the choices that are made in life are true, honest and fair.

Palm Sunday, towards the end of Lent, begins Holy Week, commemorating the day when Jesus entered Jerusalem with his disciples. Maundy Thursday commemorates the Last Supper and betrayal of Jesus. Many Christians celebrate with Eucharist on this day. Then they may remove things from the altar or communion table to remind them of Jesus being betrayed and taken from them. Good Friday is a day of mourning for the crucifixion when Christians worship in silent, bare churches. On Holy Saturday special services may be held during the night, as this was when the resurrection took place. When the women came to the tomb on the Sunday morning it was empty. On Easter Sunday the churches are therefore bright with flowers, lights and music. Christians rejoice in the belief of the

A Good Friday procession, remembering Jesus' journey to the cross

resurrection and divinity of Jesus, and the promise of eternal life.

What part does pilgrimage play in Christianity?

Pilgrimage is not compulsory in Christianity, but ever since early times Christians have made journeys to places associated with the story of Jesus and the **saints**.

Christians regard all of the land of Israel as the Holy Land, but the most important holy sites are in Jerusalem where Jesus died and was resurrected. Every Easter pilgrims gather at the hill of Calvary where Jesus was crucified and thank God for sending His Son.

Some Christians make pilgrimage in the hope of receiving some spiritual blessing or healing. At Lourdes in France there is a spring of water which is believed to have healing powers. In England Christians often walk over 100 miles to shrines such as Walsingham, in Norfolk, during Holy Week to remember the last week of Jesus' life and his journey to the cross.

What is the Christian life?

Christians seek to live in a way that brings them closer to God. They regard Jesus as the perfect expression of God's nature in human terms. The ideal they seek to follow, therefore, is that which is provided by the life and teachings of Jesus.

What do Christians seek to achieve?

Christians seek to make sure that the world actually operates in the way that God intended. They try to achieve this through prayer, action in the world and the way they live their lives.

Why is love so important for Christians?

Jesus reminded people that the greatest commandment was to love God with all one's soul, mind and strength, and that the second was to love one's neighbour as oneself (see Dt 6:5 or Lev 19:18). Christians believe that to love God means also to love people.

In what ways do Christians express their love?

Prayer and worship are important, but so too is active involvement with the world through, for example:

- working to help the poor and oppressed people
- upholding the principles of family life and sexual morality
- questioning the way we live in the world
- joining the struggle for peace in the world
- showing compassion to those who suffer and the needy.

This newly-married Christian couple receive a blessing from the priest

The Blessed Virgin Mary and the infant Jesus

? Questions

1 From what does the name 'Christian' come?

2 Describe the main beliefs of Christians.

3 On what public occasions might a Creed be used?

4 Name the main places where Christian worship takes place.

5 Explain what is meant by the term 'salvation'.

6 Explain why Eucharist is an important part of Christian worship. What does it mean to Christians? Give an account of the differences of opinion that different Christian groups have about the Eucharist.

7 *'Jesus may have been a very brave and good man. But he failed to make any major changes and bring peace on Earth.'* What points might a Christian make in response to this statement?

2 Islam

☪ Islam: Essential Facts

Origins	Seventh century CE, Arabia
Present spread	Gulf States, Africa, Bangladesh, Pakistan, USA, Europe
Prophets	Muhammad (Peace be upon him*)
Major beliefs	Shahadah, Tawhid, Angels, Prophets, Day of Judgement
Sacred writings	The Qur'an, Hadith
Special places of worship	Masjid (Mosque)
Special times	Eid-ul-Fitr, Eid-ul-Adha, Ramadan, Muharram, Day of Arafat, Muhammad's birthday
Religious teachers	Imam who lead the communal prayers, but there are no priests as such
Places of pilgrimage	Makkah (Mecca)
Holy day	Friday
Forms of worship	Prayers five times each day, reading the Qur'an, Sawm (Fasting during Ramadan), Hajj (Pilgrimage) and Zakah (Almsgiving)
Groups	Sunni, Shi'ite, Kharijites, Sufis

* 'Peace be upon him' is what a devout Muslim would normally say

 **Origins of Islam**

What is Islam?

Islam is often used as a name for a religion which draws its inspiration from the revelations to the prophet **Muhammad** who lived in Arabia in the seventh century. It is one of the most widespread of religions. Followers of Islam are called **Muslims** and they now number about 800 million worldwide.

In Arabic, the word **Islam** means peace and submission and can even mean 'I surrender'. So someone who follows Islam is someone who is seeking to become peaceful, submissive and willing to surrender to the will of **Allah** (the name of God in Islam). Islam in this sense is a way of life.

Who was Muhammad?

Muslims believe that many prophets or teachers have been sent by Allah, including Moses and Jesus Christ, but that Muhammad was the greatest of them all – 'The seal of the prophets'. He was born in **Makkah** about 570 CE. In around 610 CE, Muslims believe that he received revelations from Allah through the Angel Jibril which he was to pass on to his fellow Makkans. These messages or revelations were later collected and form the **Qur'an**. The teachings of the Islamic religion are based on the Qur'an. Stories about his life and work are recorded in the **Hadith** which has become an additional source of inspiration for Muslims.

Qur'an and Kursi (stool)

What is the Hijrah?

Muhammad and his followers were persecuted in Makkah. In 622 CE, they left the city and went to **al-Madinah**. This is the celebrated **Hijrah**, or 'emigration', the event from which the Muslim calendar begins. Muhammad gained many followers in al-Madinah and the city became a Muslim community ruled by the revelations given to the prophet.

By 630 CE, Muhammad had gathered an army strong enough to conquer Makkah. By now, a number of Arab tribes had accepted his message and slowly Arabia was being united by his teachings. Muhammad died in 632 CE, and was succeeded by a number of Caliphs ('successors').

What did Muhammad achieve?

- The establishment of Muslim religious practice and belief.
- The destruction of idolatry (the worshipping of idols) and polytheism (belief in more than one god) among his people.
- The uniting of warring tribes into one religious community.
- The start of the struggle to establish the rule of Allah in the world.

What happened after Muhammad's death?

After Muhammad died in 632 CE, there was no obvious successor and this resulted in a difference of opinion between two groups about how the leader should be chosen. One group declared that the leader should be chosen by the community. The other held that only Allah could choose the leader. The first group believed that Allah intended Muhammad's son-in-law, Ali, to be the leader, but the other party chose Abu Bakr as the Caliph. The followers of Ali became known as **Shi'ites**, and the followers of Abu Bakr as the **Sunni**. The best known descendents of the Shi'ites are the Iranian Muslims led by the Ayatollahs.

The Sunni were the largest and most powerful group, as they still are today. They founded the Umayyad Dynasty (661-750 CE) which extended the borders of the Islamic empire westward to Spain and eastward to India. Islamic influence in Spain ended in the fifteenth century, and in the nineteenth century it lost ground in Eastern Europe, though small pockets of Muslims can be found, like the Kosovo Albanians.

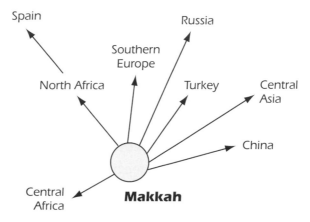

The spread of Islam from the seventh to the fourteenth century

The symmetry of the mosque expresses Tawhid

What is the view of God in Islam?

Muslims refer to God as Allah and they believe in one God. The word 'Muslim' means one who lives his life according to the Will of Allah. Muslims have 99 names for Allah which they chant as a form of prayer.

Tawhid is an important Muslim belief. It expresses the unity of Allah, that He is All-powerful and is the Creator of all that exists. He has no partner or equal, nor does He take on a human form. Islam does not accept that Jesus is the Son of God but does say that he was a prophet. The Qur'an insists that only Allah is worthy of worship. Muhammad is viewed as a person who was charged with a special mission from Allah. This belief in the oneness of Allah is expressed in the **Shahadah**:

> 'There is no god but Allah and Muhammad is the messenger of Allah.'

Muslims may repeat the Shahadah to themselves many times throughout their daily lives.

Who are the servants of Allah?

Muslims believe that prophets have been sent to all nations. Among these prophets were Abraham, Moses, Noah and Jesus.

Muslims also believe in the existence of angels, who perform certain duties entrusted to them by Allah. They also believe in spiritual beings called **jinn**. Their purpose is to serve or worship Allah. Rebellious jinn are called demons. The chief demon is **Iblis** or Satan, whom Allah allows to tempt men and women to evil.

Muslims have adopted the stars and the moon as symbols for their belief that Islam guides and illuminates humans on the journey of life

Why are peace and submission so important for Muslims?

Muslims believe that we will only find peace when we realise that nothing which happens on Earth is independent of Allah. If people forget this and try to live independent lives, they will lose their sense of peace. The true Muslim freely submits to Allah's purpose and is at peace in knowing that they carry out the way of life for which they were created.

What are the five pillars of Islam?

The **five pillars of Islam** are the most important rules according to which Muslims seek to live. They are:

A prayer mat used for Salah

- **Confession of Faith** (Shahadah) – The repeated profession of belief in one Allah and in Muhammad as Allah's messenger.
- **Ritual Prayer** (**Salah**) – Muslims pray five times daily and Muslim men should attend the Jumu'ah prayers on a Friday.
- **Fasting** (**Sawm**) – During the month of **Ramadan** Muslims must not eat, drink, smoke or have sexual relations between dawn and sunset.
- **Almsgiving** (**Zakah**) – Giving alms (charitable donations) to support the poor and needy is regarded as a religious duty.
- **Pilgrimage** (**Hajj**) – Every Muslim is required to go to Makkah at least once in their lifetime.

In addition to the pillars, there is **Jihad**, the struggle to establish the rule of Allah in ourselves and others. One meaning of Jihad is to defend Islam. It takes many other forms such as learning, good works and self-control.

 **The Qur'an**

What is the Qur'an?

The Qur'an is the last revelation and the culmination of all previous sacred writings (scriptures), including the Bible. Muslims believe that the words existed in heaven from the beginning and were then revealed to Muhammad and later recorded in the exact way that he received them:

> 'The Qur'an is no other than revelation revealed to him (Muhammad): One terrible power taught it him Endowed with Wisdom.'
> (The Qur'an, Surah 53)

Why is the Qur'an important for Muslims?

Muslims believe that they require a pattern of life which places Allah at the centre of everything they do. The Qur'an is the guidance for their life. In one sense it provides a set of rules to follow. But it is also more than this because Muslims believe that it has the power to change a person's life. Many Muslims recite from the Qur'an every day, for example, and believe that this helps them to achieve a sense of physical and spiritual completeness and closeness to their Creator.

How do Muslims show respect for the Qur'an?

They show their respect in various ways. When it is being read or recited, for example, everyone is silent and may not eat or drink. When the book is not being read it is wrapped in a clean cloth and kept on a shelf above all other books. It is kept on a special stand and great ceremony is attached to it when it is taken out for prayer or study. However, the most important way of showing respect for Allah is to learn the Qur'an by heart so as to be able to recite it at will. Muslims who achieve this are recognised by the title '**hafiz**' being attached as an addition to their name, eg Hafiz Iqbal Aftab.

The Qur'an was revealed to Muhammad in Arabic, and is still written in that language. This means that it cannot be changed or misinterpreted.

Young Muslims learning Arabic to read the Qur'an

What is the Hadith?

This contains various accounts about the life and activities of Muhammad that passed among Muslims after his death. The most reliable accounts became known as **Sunnah** (custom), the example set by Muhammad's own life which all Muslims should follow. There are several Hadith collections and they elaborate on the rules given in the Qur'an on all aspects of life.

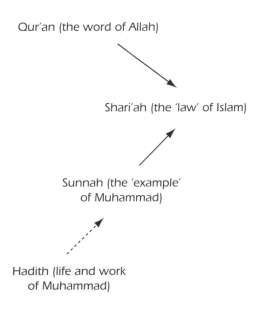

Qur'an (the word of Allah)

Shari'ah (the 'law' of Islam)

Sunnah (the 'example' of Muhammad)

Hadith (life and work of Muhammad)

Worship in Islam

How do Muslims worship?

Muslims may pray alone or with other Muslims. However, even when they pray alone in their home or workplace they are aware of the whole community of Muslims praying together. All Muslims will be facing Makkah and all will be performing the  same actions and words. At the end of the prayer session, each worshipper will turn to the right and the left to acknowledge their fellow worshippers.

What is the mosque?

A masjid

The Muslim place of public worship is the **masjid** (mosque). Masjids can vary greatly in shape and size, from magnificent structures on a grand scale to the plainest, most basic of buildings. However, they share a number of fundamental features. These include an enclosed hall, where Muslim's kneel, sit or prostrate themselves before Allah to perform their prayer; an opening or niche (**mihrab**) in an interior wall that indicates the direction of

Makkah which worshippers must face when praying; a pulpit (**minbar**) from which the sermon is spoken; and, in most countries, a minaret or tower, situated outside the masjid, from which a person known as the **Mu'adhin** calls Muslims to prayer.

On special occasions a sermon is preached in the masjid from the minbar

There are no pictures or statues in the masjid. Muslims regard pictures and statues as a distraction from the purpose of prayer, which is to concentrate on Allah. No pictures or images can adequately portray Allah.

What is Salah?

This is the Arabic term for the ritual prayer that is the centre of Muslim worship. There are five prayer times, each preceded by ritual washing – before dawn, after midday, mid-afternoon, after sunset and night. Praying five times a day in a regular and disciplined manner serves to remind Muslims of their status before Allah as 'worshipful servants'.

The act of ritual washing (**Wudu**) prepares the Muslim to appear before Allah in a clean and refreshed state. It is both a mark of respect for Allah and a way of preparing body and mind for Salah.

The ritual prayer is not just spoken, but made with rhythmic bodily movements as well. Bowing is one of the main movements. **Rak'ah** refers to the number of times Muslims repeat the action of bowing during the prayer. The number of Rak'ahs varies between two and four depending on which of the five daily prayers is being performed.

Another key movement in the Salah is when Muslims lower their forehead so that it touches the ground. This is known as **Sujdah** or 'prostration' in English. Muslims regard it as a symbol of total submission to Allah.

Why do Muslims pray?

There are several reasons:

- Because Allah has instructed His followers to pray.
- It is a way of praising and glorifying Allah.
- Prayer is one way Muslims express submission to the Will of Allah.
- It is necessary to pray in order to receive Allah's blessing and seek forgiveness.
- Muslims say they do not pray in order to influence Allah, but in order to change themselves.

Muslim men performing Wudu, before going in to pray

 ## Islamic Law

What is the Shari'ah?

Central to Islam is the idea that the life of each Muslim and of the Islamic community should be guided by the will of Allah. Muslims refer to the Qur'an and the Hadith to decide how they should conduct their lives. However, the Qur'an does not provide detailed guidance on every point. It has been necessary for the Muslim community, the **Ummah**, to interpret the relevant verses in the Qur'an and other sacred scriptures. In this way, a system of laws and rules has been formulated over the centuries. The system is called the **Shari'ah**.

What does Shari'ah mean?

Shari'ah is based on the Arabic word for 'path'. It is viewed as a path that leads from Allah and to Allah. The interpreters of the sacred law are the Ulama. They study the law in great detail and know a lot about all areas of Islamic teaching.

The Shari'ah covers all aspects of human life, not just religious duties. It provides a code by which Muslims conduct their economic, social, political and personal relationships.

Traditionally, all government laws in Muslim countries were based on the Shari'ah. Today, however, these countries vary in the extent to which they apply the sacred laws.

What does the sacred law require?

Customary practices encouraged by the sacred law include:

- Husband and wife have individual rights and responsibilities.
- Muslims should behave kindly and with consideration towards others and especially their parents.
- They should remember the poor, orphans and the needy.
- They should be patient and honest, and be tolerant to non-believers.
- Extramarital relations are forbidden.

- Men and women should dress modestly so as not to show the shape of the body.

Muslim women dressed modestly talking to a visitor to an exhibition

- Certain foods, such as pig meats, must not be eaten. The slaughter of animals for human consumption must be carried out according to carefully followed ritual (**halal**).

Food must be prepared according to strict requirements

- Alcohol is not allowed.
- Gambling is not allowed.
- Muslims have a particular responsibility (**khalifah**) for looking after the natural world.

Special Times and Pilgrimage

What are the main special times in Islam?

The Muslim calendar dates from the Hijrah and is calculated according to the Moon. This means that a year is slightly shorter than in the western calendar. As a result of this, festivals move throughout the seasons. The Muslim name for a special time is **eid** or **id**. The two principal festivals are:

- **Ramadan** and **Eid-ul-Fitr** Ramadan is the third pillar of Islam. It is the name of the ninth month of the Muslim calendar, and during this month Muslims go without food and drink during daylight hours. Ramadan recalls the revelation of the Qur'an. Especially important is Laylat-ul-Qadr, the Night of Power, when all Muslims try to worship. Ramadan helps Muslims overcome selfish desires. Eid-ul-Fitr marks the end of Ramadan. It is the first day of Shawwal, the tenth month of the Muslim year. It is an enjoyable and pleasant occasion: presents are given, family and friends are visited, and special prayers are said at the masjid. The **Imam** reminds Muslims that they must give the value of a full meal to charity; this is sadaqat-ul-fitr, and the money is usually given before the feast so that all can eat well on the feast day.

- **Eid-ul-Adha** marks the end of the annual pilgrimage to Makkah. It is also known as the Great Feast and the Festival of Sacrifice. It recalls how Ibrahim was willing to sacrifice his son as an act of complete submission to Allah. There are special prayers and traditionally an animal is sacrificed to provide a special meal. The sacrifice symbolises the giving of oneself to Allah.

What is Hajj?

This is the pilgrimage to Makkah. The fifth of the five pillars of Islam requires that the pilgrimage be fulfilled at least once in a lifetime if possible. The most holy of holy places for Muslims are to be found at Makkah and its surrounding area. These places are associated with Muhammad who began his life and ministry at Makkah.

The pilgrimage takes place during the twelfth month, Dhul-Hijjah, of the Muslim year. Every Muslim is expected to make the pilgrimage to Makkah at least once in their lifetime, providing that they are in good health and can afford it. More than two million Muslims from around the world and from all walks of life travel to Makkah to make the pilgrimage each year. Once in Makkah the pilgrims follow a set route around the holy sites.

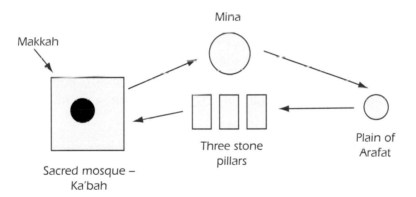

The Plain of Arafat is the place where Allah showed mercy to Isma'il the son of Ibrahim. The three stone pillars symbolise the devil's temptation of Isma'il and in throwing stones at the pillars, Muslims show their willingness to defeat evil and allow good to triumph.

What is the religious meaning of Hajj?

- It is an expression of the unity of all Muslims from around the world. At any Hajj there will be representatives from almost every country in which Muslims live.

- It is a sign of dutiful obedience and faith. During the Hajj, the Muslim is at the disposal of Allah and must be able to observe all the conditions and rituals.
- It strengthens individual faith and identity with the worldwide Muslim community.
- It is a focus for the whole of a Muslim's life and belief.
- It symbolises their equality – they all wear the same type of simple clothes and perform the same rituals; all are the same before Allah.

What is the Ka'bah?

The **Ka'bah** is a large cube-shaped building in Makkah. It has a sacred black stone built into the eastern corner. It is a meeting point for Muslims from all over the world and symbolises their unity. Visiting the Ka'bah is one of the most important moments of Hajj. According to the Qur'an, the prophet Ibrahim built the Ka'bah, helped by his son, Isma'il, as a sign of their submission to Allah. Muslims believe that the Ka'bah was the first building devoted to the worship of the one true God, Allah. When pilgrims visit the Ka'bah they make a ceremonial journey round it known as **tawaf**.

A picture of the Ka'bah.
Most Muslim homes will have such a picture

☪ Islam Today

How is Islam affected by western culture?

Since 1945 CE Islamic countries have been increasingly exposed to the influences of liberalism and capitalism. This has meant that they have increasingly had to confront the dilemma of whether to accept or reject this capitalist culture.

There has been a variety of responses to this problem. Some countries, such as Iran and Libya, have generally adopted an Islamic way of life for their population and in their relations with other countries. In other countries, such as Turkey and Tunisia, a process of secularisation has been occurring whereby

Trainee priests visit a mosque

religion is separated from politics and little attempt is made to prevent the influence of capitalism. Still others, such as Saudi Arabia and the Gulf States, have preserved Islamic institutions but have also developed close links with capitalist nations.

? Questions

1 What is the origin of the name 'Islam'?
2 What are the five main beliefs that Muslims share?
3 Explain the meaning of the term 'Jihad'.
4 Write as a Muslim explaining the value of praying five times a day.
5 Explain how fasting during Ramadan can help Muslims overcome selfish desires.
6 Give five reasons why the Hajj helps Muslims feel that they are members of a worldwide community.

3 Judaism

✡ Judaism: Essential Facts

Origins	c1900 BCE, the Mediterranean countries
Present spread	Israel, Russia, USA, western Europe
Prophets	Abraham, Moses, David, Solomon, Amos, Isaiah, and many others
Major beliefs	The covenant; the unity of G-d; judgement and repentance; the Ten Commandments; the Law (Torah)
Sacred writings	Torah, Talmud
Special places of worship	Home and synagogue
Special times	Rosh Hashanah, Yom Kippur, Pesach, Shavuot, Sukkot, Purim
Religious teachers	Rabbis
Places of pilgrimage	The Western Wall, Masada, Yad Vashem
Holy day	Shabbat (Friday sunset to Saturday sunset)
Forms of worship	Psalms and thanksgiving, prayers, study and readings from sacred texts, celebrations, rituals, the wearing of tefillin and tallit
Groups	Orthodox, Conservative, Reform and Liberal

✡ Origins of Judaism

What is Judaism?

Judaism is the religion of the Jewish people. Religious Jews believe that they are the descendants of Abraham and the Israelites, whose stories are told in the **Torah** (the Five Books of the **Hebrew** Bible). They believe that G-d revealed His teaching to Abraham and later to the Israelites, and that He chose them and their descendants (the Jewish people) to be a light or example to all humanity.

The Star of David – The six points stand for G-d, the Word and Man, and G-d's three great acts of Creation, Revelation and Redemption

What is the Covenant?

At the heart of Judaism is the belief in one G-d who, more than 4000 years ago, appeared to Abraham and made a covenant or special agreement with him. By this agreement, Abraham and his descendants promised to obey G-d's laws by living righteously and justly. In

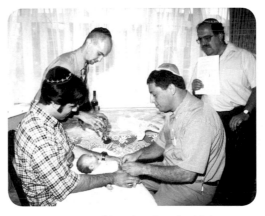

Circumcision taking place in a Jewish home

return, G-d promised to give them the land of Canaan (also known as Palestine and Israel) and to make them His chosen people. The act of **circumcision** (**Brit Milah**), the removal of the foreskin from the penis of each male, became the sign of this special covenant.

According to the Torah, G-d appeared to Abraham and said, '*I will make you into a great nation*' (Gn 12:2). Jews interpret this as meaning that G-d wants them to be a great nation in an ethical and religious sense. To achieve this they must live as a moral community which follows closely and rigorously G-d's teachings. They should seek to be an example and inspiration to others.

Who was Moses?

Abraham's descendants became known as Israelites. Moses was a great leader who led the Israelites out of Egyptian slavery around 1250 BCE. This is known as the **Exodus**. At Mount Sinai, G-d appeared to Moses and reaffirmed and extended the covenant. In this covenant G-d informed the Israelites that they were to be a 'Kingdom of priests' who served the only true G-d. They were also to be a 'holy nation' who reflected the character of that G-d in their personal, social and material life. Moses also received G-d's law for the people in the form of the **Ten Commandments** (see Ex 19-20).

What was the diaspora?

The Israelites settled in the land of Canaan and made Jerusalem their religious centre. Solomon built the first temple and made it the focus of the Jewish religion. Around 70 CE, however, the Romans took possession of the Jewish lands and destroyed the temple in Jerusalem. To escape Roman rule, many Jews fled and set up new homes throughout the Mediterranean countries. This is known as the Jewish dispersion (**diaspora**).

Why do Jews believe that they are a single people?

Although Jews live in many different countries around the world, they think of themselves as a single people or nation. Religious Jews believe that they can trace their ancestry back to Abraham and the Israelites, and that in this sense they are a nation. The covenant is based on the idea of the Jews as a single people who have received G-d's blessing as a 'holy nation'. The feeling of being a single people which Jews share is further strengthened by the focus on the land of Israel as a spiritual home and a centre of Jewish national life.

✡ Jewish Beliefs

What does Judaism teach about G-d?

Belief that there is only one G-d (monotheism) is central to Judaism. G-d is seen as the creator and ruler of the world. He is transcendent (outside or above the physical laws of the universe) and eternal. He sees everything and knows everything.

Judaism holds that G-d is a unity. He has no agent or incarnation of himself. Judaism teaches that the name of the divine is **Yahweh**. Jews do not pronounce the sacred name, but instead they use the word **Lord**. Out of respect for Jewish beliefs we are using G-d in this section.

The Torah teaches that G-d led His people out of slavery in Egypt. Jews believe that this shows that G-d is all-powerful, merciful and loving, and that the Jews are His chosen people. It also proves that G-d keeps His promises to His people, and that in return Jews should be loyal and obedient to His Law.

Jewish beliefs and practices are found in the Torah

In what sense does G-d speak?

One of the most distinctive characteristics of Judaism is the belief in a G-d who speaks and acts in the world. Jews believe that G-d reveals Himself to His people through spoken commands. The Torah, for example, describes how G-d revealed Himself to Moses and promised that He would free the Israelites from the Egyptians. The Hebrew scriptures then show how G-d acted to deliver what He promised. For example, He commanded the Red Sea to part to allow the Israelites to make their escape. Thus Judaism encourages belief in the sovereign power of G-d's Word. G-d has a purpose or plan for His people which He communicates to them through spoken instructions and declarations. Always G-d's Word accomplishes what it says will happen.

41

How does G-d speak to His people?

G-d speaks to His people through a number of sources:

- **Prophets** – They are regarded as people near to G-d. Their primary task is to deliver G-d's message to His people at a particular point in time and this may sometimes include predictions of what the future will hold. Moses was the greatest of the prophets, for it was to him alone that G-d's laws (The Ten Commandments) were revealed. Lesser prophets include Samuel, Amos and Daniel.

- **Priests** – The **rabbi** is the teacher and interpreter of G-d's law. Their interpretation is known as **Midrash**. Other people may also act as ministers, but they may not be qualified as a rabbi.

- **Wise people** – Their worldly experience is the basis of a special understanding of what G-d requires.

- **Ordinary people** – People can hear what G-d is saying through prayer, meditation, and by following the Commandments.

What is the Law of G-d?

Religious Jews seek to love G-d with their whole being and they express that love through obedience to the Law of G-d in everyday life. It teaches that the Law of G-d is revealed to people in the Torah and other sacred writings, and through the interpretations of rabbis and wise men.

The Torah is said to contain 613 commandments covering every area of daily life from civil laws to personal hygiene and diet. It expresses in a practical way how the Jew is to seek G-d and relate to Him in the everyday business of life. In short, it provides rules for a complete way of life.

Jews praying in a home after a circumcision

What are the Ten Commandments?

The Ten Commandments provide a summary of G-d's Law.
The Torah describes how G-d gave the commandments to
Moses, saying:

> 'I am the Lord your G-d, who brought you out of Egypt, out of the
> land of slavery. You shall have no other g-ds before me.' (Ex 20:2-3)

In summary, the Ten Commandments are:

- Worship G-d alone
- Do not make any images of G-d
- Do not use G-d's name for evil purposes
- Keep the Sabbath day holy
- Respect your father and mother
- Do not murder
- Do not commit adultery
- Do not steal
- Do not accuse anyone falsely
- Do not desire another man's possessions

What are the Noachide Laws?

As well as the Ten Commandments, Jews also base their moral
behaviour on the seven commandments given to Noah after the
flood. The Noachide Laws specify that Jews must:

- not worship any G-d but Him
- not blaspheme
- not murder
- not steal
- not commit adultery
- not be cruel to animals
- establish a rule of law to live in harmony.

What are the three requirements?

One of the main concerns of Judaism is what holds people together in a society and leads them to behave well towards each other. The **Pikei Avot** ('Sayings of the Fathers') is a sacred Jewish text which teaches that human society is supported by three things: the Law, worship and deeds of kindness.

The Law is a basis for right living, it offers guidance in religion and morals. Worship is the way the believer responds to G-d, the actions they take spiritually and in their daily lives to express their commitment to G-d. Kindness is based on love and respect for justice. Jews are required to love one's neighbour as oneself, and to develop an open, warm response to others. They should also provide for the weak, show respect for the aged, care for employees, and avoid prejudice towards others.

Religious Jews believe that by showing love for G-d in everything they do, they will make life better for others in practical and spiritual ways. Daily activities, such as eating, drinking, labouring, become a celebration of G-d, and in this way people behave with gentleness, kindness and respect for others.

Central Jewish values are contained in the Ten Commandments which are represented in all synagogues

What does it mean to say that life is sacred?

Jews believe that all of life is sacred, for we are created in the image of G-d (see Gn 1:27). Our task is to obey and worship G-d in every area of life. Jews warn against the dangers of experiencing

G-d only in spiritual activities, such as prayer. This would mean that other areas of human experience are closed to G-d, and this offends the notion that G-d is the creator of our entire being. All experiences should be focused on G-d as a way of understanding His will and kindness.

What value does freedom have in Judaism?

Freedom is highly valued in Judaism. Jews believe that it has religious importance because G-d gave them their freedom at the time of the escape from slavery in Egypt. Many of the political principles and civil liberties on which western democracy is focused were originally based on Jewish religious writings.

Freedom also means for the Jews the idea that people are free to shape the future and to make progress towards a perfected society based on G-d's Law. The symbol of this freedom is found in their belief in a Messiah who will liberate them from slavery:

> *'In my vision at night I looked, and there before me was one like a son of man, coming with the clouds of heaven. He approached the Ancient of Days and was led into his presence.'*

> *'He was given authority, glory and sovereign power; all peoples, nations and men of every language worshipped him. His dominion is an everlasting dominion that will not pass away, and his kingdom is one that will never be destroyed.'*   (Dan 7:13-14)

What does Judaism teach about judgement and the after-life?

Judaism teaches that people are responsible for their actions and will be judged by G-d accordingly. Sinners must repent and mend their ways or else they will be punished in some way. Jews also believe that G-d is loving and merciful. He shows favour and forgiveness to whoever He chooses.

Traditional Jewish belief views heaven and hell as two distinct places. The departed enter one or the other to be punished or rewarded. However, many religious Jews say it is pointless to speculate about an after-life as no one can demonstrate what it will be like.

✡ Sacred Writings

What is the Jewish Bible?

The Hebrew name for the Jewish Bible is **Tenakh**. The letters TNK stand for the initial letters of the three parts of the Jewish Bible: Torah, **Nevi'im** and **Ketuvim**. It consists of books written by different authors over a thousand years. The Tenakh is the core of Judaism and religious Jews say that they live by it and always carry it in their hearts and minds.

A Jewish scroll – The book of Esther

The five books of the Tenakh – the Torah – contain the laws of Judaism and the early history of the Jewish people:

- **Genesis** is the Jewish interpretation of creation and the universe.
- **Exodus** is the escape from Egypt with Moses.
- **Leviticus** gives rules for priests and about sacrificing and leprosy.
- **Numbers** is about the wanderings of the Jews with Moses from Mount Sinai to Canaan.
- **Deuteronomy** is an account of how Jews should live, emphasising the importance of the Ten Commandments.

The main purpose of the Torah is to help Jews answer the question, *'What does G-d require?'*. This is the question which Jews are instructed to ask as part of their service to G-d and as the key to their moral values. The Torah is believed to be perfect in every respect. Its teachings must not be altered and every part is of equal importance.

What are the different parts of the Bible?

The first part is the Torah and this has the highest status. The Torah plays a key part in Jewish worship. It is also the text which Jews are expected to spend most time studying.

The **Nevi'im** (prophets) comprises books which are often divided between the major and minor prophets. There are three major prophets – Isaiah, Jeremiah and Ezekiel – and 12 minor prophets. The prophets were the great inspirers of religion and they interpreted it for the people. Jews believe that G-d specially called the prophets and gave them His message to declare. Their main task was to remind the Jews of their responsibilities towards the covenant.

The **Ketuvim** (writings) is a collection of 11 books. Some of them, such as the Book of Psalms or the Book of Proverbs, are widely used in Jewish worship. Others contain well-known religious stories. Some books stress Jewish understanding, especially Ecclesiastes, which sets out that wealth is not important and cannot last; the meaning of life is beyond human understanding.

What other sacred writings are recognised in Judaism?

After the Torah, the **Talmud** is Judaism's most cherished book. Talmud means 'teaching' and it contains instructions for following a Jewish way of life and understanding Jewish laws.

The Talmud consists of two parts, the **Mishnah** and the **Gemara**. The Mishnah provides guidance on a number of subjects including the rights of the poor, the role of priests, marriage and divorce, diet, and ritual laws. The Gemara is a commentary on how to interpret the laws outlined in the Mishnah. It combines stories with a moral (**Agadah**) with details of the laws (**Halakhah**).

Devout Jews regard Judaism as a complete way of life and this is reflected in their sacred writings which provide detailed guidance on virtually all aspects of behaviour, including marriage and divorce, the rights of the poor, the role of the priests, civil and criminal law, diet, and relations with friends and neighbours.

A Jewish wedding in a synagogue

The Midrash are writings based on sermons by rabbis (see page 50). They provide a way of interpreting the inner meaning of the stories in the Torah.

What is the Zohar?

These are a collection of ancient writings that have become the Holy Book of the **Kabbalah** – the mystical tradition of Judaism. The writings are attributed to Rabbi Simeon bar Yochai, a second-century CE teacher from Palestine.

What is the synagogue?

The **synagogue** is the centre of public worship and community life for religious Jews. It is normally a purpose-built building. Prayer, study and special family occasions such as weddings and **Bar** and **Bat Mitzvahs** (see page 52) take place here.

The synagogue is a place of worship, study, where Jews, especially children, receive religious instruction, and also a place where Jews meet.

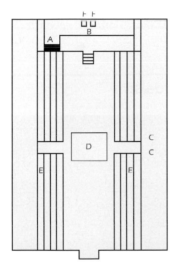

Plan of a synagogue

A   Seat of the rabbi

B   Ark (**Aron Hakodesh**) with scrolls of the Torah

C   Gallery

D   Central pulpit for scripture reading and sermons

E   Pews

F   Two plaques with the Ten Commandments written on them

Inside a synagogue

What is Shabbat?

Shabbat, or the Sabbath as it is known in English, is the Jewish day of worship and rest. It lasts from Friday sunset to Saturday sunset. Shabbat is holy because it commemorates G-d's rest on the seventh day of creation and reminds Jews of the deliverance from Egypt. This is a central commandment of Judaism.

> *'Observe the Sabbath day by keeping keep it holy, as the Lord your G-d has commanded you.'* (Dt 5:12)

Each week the Shabbat is celebrated with a festival that centres on the home as well as the synagogue. The main acts of worship take place in the synagogue on Friday evening and Saturday morning, and in the home on Friday and Saturday evenings.

> *'Six days you shall labour and do all your work, but the seventh day is a Sabbath to the Lord your G-d.'* (Ex 20:9-10)

What is the role of the rabbi in Judaism?

The rabbi is a religious leader in the community and a source of authority. The term 'rabbi' literally means teacher. The rabbi can issue Agadah, which are teachings on the moral code. He also leads prayers in the synagogue and at weddings and funerals.

Not all Jewish communities are served by a rabbi. Some may have a minister who is not a rabbi.

The Ark in a Jewish synagogue

What part does prayer play in Judaism?

A devout Jew prays three times a day – morning, afternoon and evening. When a Jewish man prays, he covers his head with an ordinary hat or a skull cap (**kippah**). Some Jewish men cover their head at all times. On days other than Shabbat and Yom Tov (high holy days) he will wear a **tallit** (prayer shawl) and **tefillin**, which are bound on his head and arm.

Kippah

In Judaism, prayers need not be restricted to the synagogue or the home since worship may be offered anywhere. The crucial point is that G-d is approached in a spirit of respect and humility. This means that worshippers should be open to G-d and ready to listen to what He is saying to them. Their mind should not be elsewhere as this would be irreverent and mock G-d's power.

A Jew praying with kippah, tallit and tefillin

Prayers are regarded as valuable by Jews in that they enable them to understand G-d better. They also provide an opportunity for the offering of praise and petitions (requests) to G-d when necessary.

Shema

The daily prayer of Judaism – The **Shema**:

> 'Hear, O Israel, The Lord our G-d, the Lord is one; Love the Lord your G-d with all your heart and with all your soul and with all your strength. These commandments that I give you today are to be upon your hearts. Impress them on your children. Talk about them when you sit at home and when you walk along the road, when you lie down and when you get up. Tie them as symbols on your hands and bind them on your foreheads. Write them on the doorframes of your houses and on your gates.' (Dt 6:4-9)

What part does the home play in Jewish religious life?

The home is the centre of Jewish religious life – even more than the synagogue. Children begin their religious education here. Verses from the Torah should be nailed to the doorposts of all the main doors of the house, written on a tiny scroll and sealed in a narrow container called a **mezuzah**. It is usual for the verses which instruct the Shema to be found in the mezuzah placed on the doorposts.

Mezuzah

The mother plays a key role in preserving the faith and ensuring that it is practised regularly in the home. On Friday evening as the Shabbat begins she lights the Shabbat candles and prays for G-d's blessing on her work and her family. This is followed by a special family meal, songs and prayers. Parents bless their children and the father recites the Prayer of Sanctification (**Kiddush**).

The home is the place where **kosher** foods – those considered 'fit' for Jews to eat because they are ritually clean – are prepared. Milk and meat dishes are kept totally separate from each other in accordance with the instruction given in the Torah. Some Jews also believe that kosher laws stem from the need for a healthy diet.

Why do Jews consider that religious study is very important?

One reason is that religious study is a sign of humility and reverence; it shows willingness to learn and follow G-d's Law. Education is also important because the Law covers every area of life. Systematic study is required in order to know and understand the Law.

The synagogue is a place of study ('a home of learning') where Jews, especially children, receive religious education. The ceremonies of Bar Mitzvah and Bat Mitzvah make boys and girls sons or daughters of the Law. Young Jews need to study the Torah in great detail before they are ready to claim this title.

Special Times and Pilgrimage

The Jewish Year

The Jewish year is regulated by a cycle of festivals and commemorations which are central to Judaism. They are communal events which forge a link between Judaism past and present, and focus on the central beliefs of the faith.

What is Rosh Hashanah?

The Jewish year begins with the seventh month (Tishri) and is celebrated by Jews all over the world in the festival known as **Rosh Hashanah** (New Year). It is the time when Jewish people remember their Creator and what He has done for them. They reflect on His judgement on evil and by repenting their sins they begin the New Year by submitting to Him. It is a quiet day of solemn reflection.

What is Yom Kippur?

Yom Kippur (Day of Atonement) is the holiest of Jewish festivals with 24 hours of fasting to show sincerity, self-discipline, dedication and compassion. It is a public act of reconciliation with G-d which commemorates their faithlessness in the wilderness (see Lv 16). On this day the Ark is covered in white and a solemn prayer (Kol Nidrei) is sung as a memorial to Jews who have suffered persecution. Sins are confessed directly to G-d and prayers are said for forgiveness for personal and private wrongs.

What is Pesach?

Pesach is also known as Passover. It celebrates the deliverance of the Israelites from slavery in Egypt when they were led to freedom by Moses after the intervention of G-d.

A Seder plate, with special places for the food used to remember how G-d saved the Israelites from slavery

The festival lasts eight days and begins with a special meal known as the **Seder**. Special food is eaten which helps Jews today identify with the suffering and joy of their ancestors.

What other special times are celebrated by Jews?

- **Shavuot** (Feast of Weeks) – Harvest festival in early summer which celebrates the revelation of the Torah to Moses at Sinai. It is also a time when special emphasis is placed upon the religious education of children.
- **Sukkot** (Feast of Tabernacles) – Nine-day autumn harvest festival. It celebrates the care received from G-d while the Jewish people wandered for 40 years in the wilderness. Jews build temporary shelters (tabernacles) of branches in their gardens, and all meals are taken there.
- **Purim** (Feast of Lots) – Early spring festival commemorating the victory of Esther over persecutors who sought to slaughter the Jews in Persia. There is a carnival atmosphere with special meals, plays portraying the story of Esther, and processions with children in fancy dress.
- **Hanukkah** – An eight-day festival of lights. Jews recall the miracle when the oil lasted in the temple lights for eight days, when there was only enough oil for a single day. Lights are lit on a special nine-branched candlestick (hanukiah). The festival also recalls the rededication of the temple after it had been desecrated.

Hanukiah

What part does pilgrimage play in Judaism?

Followers of Judaism are under no obligation to make a pilgrimage. However, Jerusalem attracts Jews from all over the world to visit holy places associated with their religion and nation.

The Western Wall in Jerusalem is a special holy place for Jews. It is the last relic of the first temple built by Solomon and has also been called 'the wailing wall' because pilgrims are sometimes overcome by grief as they stand before it.

Jews praying at the Western Wall in Jerusalem

Other places of pilgrimage for Jews in Jerusalem include Yad Vashem which is a memorial to the victims of the Holocaust and Masada which is the site of a fortress heroically defended by a small group of Jews against the Romans in 73 CE. Masada is a symbol to Jews of the extreme determination to survive as a people and to keep their faith.

✡ Community Life

Where are the main Jewish communities?

The common identity which Jews share as a religious and cultural group is based on following a similar life pattern. It is estimated that there are 13 million Jewish people in the world today. Of these, five million live in Israel. Most of the others live in Europe and North America, though Jewish communities can be found in most parts of the world.

There have been communities of Jews in Britain since 1656 CE. Many came here as refugees from religious persecution. However, the Jewish community has been declining in numbers and now stands at around 300 000. There are also thousands of 'secular' Jews who have no links with the religion in any outward form.

What are the main divisions within Judaism?

Judaism is not a unified religion today and Jews follow different traditions and customs in different parts of the world. Broadly, there are three main divisions:

Interior of a modern synoagogue

- Orthodox
- Reform
- Conservative.

Orthodox Jews follow the Law (Torah) strictly and they are opposed to any changes which they believe would undermine their faith. Reform Judaism developed at the end of the eighteenth century and blended modern scholarship with the rejection of what was, to them, outdated laws. Together with Conservative Judaism, which arose in the United States a century later, they adopted new customs, such as shorter services, allowing men and women to sit together in synagogues, the use of more English in services, modified dietary laws and new prayers.

Orthodox Judaism is the dominant form of religion in Israel, though the Reform movement is growing. In Britain, about 25% of Jews are Reform.

What is the state of Israel?

The modern state of Israel came into existence in 1948 CE. It was created in an area where there has been a Jewish settlement since ancient times. Jews from all over the world emigrated to the new state. They revived the ancient language of Hebrew as the national language of Israel.

Why was the state of Israel founded?

The Jewish people in Europe had been persecuted over many centuries. During the Second World War, they were the victims of Hitler's campaign of mass extermination. Around six million Jews died in the Nazi concentration camps. This was known as the Holocaust and led many Jews who survived to believe that only in an independent Jewish state could there be the assurance of security.

? Questions

1 What are the central beliefs of the Jewish religion?
2 Explain why Jews think of themselves as a single people or nation.
3 Explain what is meant by 'the Covenant'.
4 Why do you think the Holocaust was such a challenge to the Jewish people?
5 Jews believe that G-d is all-powerful and all-knowing. What do you think they mean?
6 *'G-d speaks to me, but not in the same way that another person might speak to me.'* How might the way that G-d speaks to people be different to the way people speak to each other?

4 Hinduism

 ## Hinduism: Essential Facts

Origins	Diverse origins in India which can be traced back thousands of years
Present spread	Mainly India and wherever migrant Indians live
Founders/Prophets	Hinduism has no named founder
Major beliefs	Brahman, atman, karma, moksha, dharma
Sacred writings	Bhagavad Gita, The Vedas, Brahmanas, Upanishads, Mahabharata, Ramayana
Special places of worship	Temples and shrines in the home
Special times	Divali, Holi, Navaratri, Dassehra (Vijay Dashami), Saraswati, Puja, Raksha Bandhan, etc
Religious teachers	Pujari, Gurus, Sadhus, Swamis
Places of pilgrimage	Dwarka, Haridwar, Varanasi (River Ganges), Vrindavan, and many other holy sites in India
Holy day	No particular day of the week is special
Forms of worship	Prayers, offerings, recital of sacred texts, ritual cleansing, etc
Sects	Vaishnaites, Shaivites, Shaktas, and more modern groups including Swaminarayan Hindu Mission and ISKCON (The International Society for Krishna Consciousness)

What is Hinduism?

Hinduism is one of the oldest and largest religions in the world. It began thousands of years ago in India, where most of its followers still live. It has no single founder or prophet, but developed gradually from early beliefs.

Today, there are many different Hindu groups or sects. They may worship the same Hindu gods, but they do not all share the same religious beliefs. Indeed, Hinduism is more like a family of religions than a single religion. It has no single scripture, no single uniting belief or set pattern of worship, nor does it have a clearly defined institutional structure.

The name 'Hindu' was first used by the ancient Persians over 2000 years ago to describe the people living near the River Indus in north-west India. However, modern Hindus prefer the phrase **Sanatan Dharma** to describe their religion. This can be translated as 'the eternal way of conduct' – eternal because it is divine in origin, and way of conduct because it covers every aspect of life.

'Om', a humming to the sounds of the letters A-U-M, is used in prayer by Hindus to symbolise the ultimate reality, Brahman

What are the origins of Hinduism?

Little is known of the origins of Hindu beliefs and practice.
Some beliefs and practices may be the result of a mixing of ideas
between the Aryan tribes who invaded India from central Asia
about 1500 BCE and the native population of India, particularly the
Indus people. The Aryan's sacred texts, known as the **Vedas**, have
exercised an important influence on the development of Hindu
beliefs and practices over the centuries.

Where do Hindus live today?

There are about 700 million Hindus in the world. The vast majority
live in India, where eight people in ten are Hindus. But there are
also Hindu communities in many other countries, including the UK,
where around 360 000 Hindus live. Although most British Hindu
families have migrated directly from India, some have come from
East Africa and other parts of the world including Trinidad and Fiji.

In the UK it is
quite common for
a Hindu temple
(**mandir**) to house
shrines to more
than one deity.
This is unlike in
India where one
building would
be dedicated to
a single god.
This means that
whatever the
family devotion
they will be able to
go to a temple to
worship and pray
to their god.

*Female worshipper bowing before
the goddess*

What do Hindus believe about God?

Many Hindus are monotheists in that they believe in the existence of one supreme soul or spirit, called **Brahman**. Brahman does not have any shape or form, but is all around, all the time, in everything. He is the origin, the cause and the basis of all existence. Many Hindus call this God.

Hindus say that Brahman is so perfect that people cannot explain or understand him. He is the unknowable one. However, the different aspects or characteristics of Brahman are manifested in various forms which people can understand. These forms are represented mostly by a range of gods and goddesses. The three main gods are **Brahma**, the creator, **Vishnu**, the protector, and **Shiva**, the destroyer and creator. Most Hindus worship Shiva, Vishnu in one of his many **avatars**, or **Shakti**, the goddess. They may regard these gods as different ways of seeing the one God (Brahman). Each male god is accompanied by its female partner, and the powers of nearly all gods and goddesses are extended by the presence of their vahana (vehicle), usually in the form of an animal or bird.

Brahman

Brahma and Saraswati   Vishnu and Lakshmi   Shiva and Parvati

Hindus gathered together to listen to a swami teaching

Brahma is seen as the creator of the universe and the god of wisdom. His female counterpart is Saraswati, the goddess of art, music and literature. Statues of Brahma often show him with four faces, embracing the four points of the compass, and with four arms, in which he holds the four Vedas (sacred writings). He is not worshipped widely as the act of creation has been completed.

Brahma

Vishnu

Vishnu, the preserver of the universe, is thought to be in charge of human fate. He is believed to incarnate himself (or to come to Earth in physical form) to rescue the world from impending chaos. Vishnu has come to Earth in many forms known as **avatars**, including a tortoise and a boar. Two in human form – Rama and Krishna – are the most widely worshipped. Vishnu is often portrayed riding on the huge eagle, Garuda, with his wife, Lakshmi, the goddess of beauty and good fortune.

Shiva is the destroyer of life. Yet also its recreator. In him there is both ceaseless activity and eternal rest. He is the source of both good and evil. In paintings and sculptures, he is often portrayed as the king of the dancers – the embodiment of cosmic energy. He is also shown with many hands, one pair to express the balance between life and death, another indicating the clash between good and evil, and so on. Shiva's wife is Parvati, the beautiful daughter of the god of the Himalayas.

Shiva

Shakti is the goddess. She is the creative energy of male gods. Myth tells how she was created from the powers of the various gods who were unable to defeat a terrifyingly evil threat. As Durga she defeated this demon and is known as 'the slayer of the buffalo demon'. She is portrayed as powerful, and yet gentle and kind, like all mothers. She is Lakshmi, the goddess of good fortune and wealth; Saraswati, the goddess of learning and music; but she is also Kali, the goddess of time, who brings both life and death to the world. Worship of the goddess is very popular, and village deities in India are always female.

Durga holding the weapons with which she protects worshippers. She is riding on her vahana, a lion

What do Hindus seek to achieve?

Hindus believe that there is a part of God in everyone. They call this **atman** or the breath of life, the inner vitality. Atman is the soul which continually strives to achieve perfection so that it can enter the eternal realm and become reunited with Brahman. When this happens, the atman and Brahman become one. Entry into eternal peace is the ultimate goal of life for Hindus and they call this **moksha**, or salvation. Some people say that atman and Brahman are the same.

What do Hindus mean by eternal peace?

Eternal peace suggests release from something felt to be undesirable, ie the cycle of rebirth and attachment to the material world. It implies a sense of calm and security, the notion of attainment (reaching a goal) or the power to be and to do at will.

What is reincarnation?

Hindus believe in reincarnation. This means that the atman is reborn in another body, human or animal, when the body dies. The same atman can be reborn many times, in a cycle of death and rebirth called **samsara**.

The aim of a Hindu's life is to break free of this cycle and to achieve moksha. Central to leading a good life is following one's **dharma**, or acting righteously and carrying out one's duty. By leading a good life, the soul can be reborn into a higher form and move closer to being united with Brahman. A bad life leads to rebirth in a lower form that is further away from the eternal. The cycle of death and rebirth is only finally broken when the person has lived such a good and holy life that their soul reaches moksha.

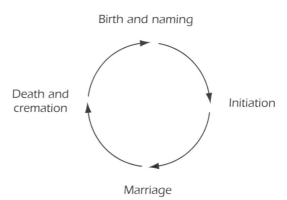

Birth and naming

Death and cremation

Initiation

Marriage

How can a Hindu achieve release from the cycle of death and rebirth?

There are four paths or ways Hindus can follow to reach moksha. They can choose whichever path is best suited to them:

- **Devotion (bhakti)** – Unquestioning faith and commitment to a particular god.
- **Right action (karma)** – Acting selflessly, without any thought of reward for themselves.
- **Knowledge (jnana)** – This has to be learned with the guidance of a religious teacher known as a **Guru** and involves reflection on the nature of God or ultimate reality.
- **Yoga (marg)** – A range of physical and mental disciplines used as aids to thinking about God. Yoga means union with God and can be applied to all the above paths, eg Bhakti-yoga is the Path of Devotion.

Krishna taught devotion to one god

ॐ Hindu Scriptures

What are the main sacred writings in Hinduism?

Hindus have a wide range of sacred writings which provide a practical guide for living and the authority for answering questions about the meaning of life and the nature of God or ultimate reality. They are used on all important occasions, including worship in the home and the temple, in private devotion and in the festivals. The scriptures were handed down orally (by word of mouth) for a long time before they were written in **Sanskrit**, the classical language of India.

There are two groups of sacred writings – **Shruti** and **Smriti**. Shruti means those that were 'heard', or received by wise men (**rishis**) through revelation or divine inspiration. Smriti means 'remembered', and refers to scriptures which contain human recollections of God's message to humankind.

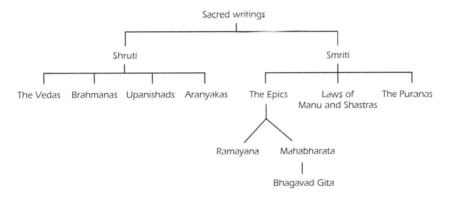

Shruti scriptures consist of:

- **The Vedas** are the earliest scriptures and comprise hymns, instructions for ritual and speculation on the nature of the ultimate reality.
- **Brahmanas** are commentaries on the Vedas, containing detailed explanations of the sacrificial rituals and symbols.
- **Upanishads** contain much of the Hindu teaching about religious and philosophical questions. They include discussion on how the soul can realise its oneness with Brahman through contemplation.

- **Aranyakas** or 'forest meditations' are supplements to the Brahmanas. They have a particularly spiritual nature and are more mystical than other writings.

Important Smriti texts include:

- **The Epics** are the great poems, **Mahabharata** and **Ramayana**. The **Bhagavad Gita**, probably the most popular Hindu holy book, is part of the Mahabharata.

- **The Laws of Manu and Shastras** (Codes of Law) are rules for regulating personal and social behaviour.

- **The Puranas** contain ancient myths about the gods and heroes of India.

What are the Great Epics?

The Ramayana and the Mahabharata are the two great epic poems of Indian literature. They are basically stories which illustrate, in a way that is easily understood, fundamental moral and religious ideas.

Sita, Rama, Lakshama and Hanuman – the heroes of the Ramayana

The Ramayana tells the story of Prince Rama and his wife, Sita. The key episode in the story is the kidnap of Sita by Ravana, King of Lanka (Sri Lanka). With the help of an army of monkeys led by Hanuman, Rama attacks Lanka and rescues Sita. The epic portrays the ideal of human virtues: Rama represents the obedient son, loving husband, dutiful king and affectionate brother. Hanuman is the ideal servant and Sita the ideal faithful wife.

The Mahabharata is divided into 18 books and is the largest epic in world religion. It contains the Bhagavad Gita which is Hinduism's most popular scripture. It teaches the virtues of service, goodness and devotion through the noble actions of Arjuna who is guided by Krishna, an incarnation of the god Vishnu.

ॐ Hindu Worship

How do Hindus worship?

Hindu worship may be expressed in words or offerings, in song and dance, or simply in silent devotion. Worship can be full of ceremony and ritual, or be very simple.

Most commonly devotion is expressed through **puja**, a type of worship involving offerings, usually of fruit and flowers. It recalls the welcome shown to an honoured guest. Additionally a light would be circled three times before the deity. This is known as the **arti** ceremony. Such offerings are a sign of reverence and respect for an honoured guest. In a temple these ceremonies would be performed by a priest. The main blessing received by the worshipper is being seen by the deity. This is known as darshan. Blessings are also received by sharing in food offered to the gods and sharing the arti lamp.

Another way of worshipping is by means of yajna (sacrifice) which is a sacred fire on which pleasant smelling substances are sprinkled as ancient religious texts are chanted.

Hindus identify with Brahman through worshipping the personal god(s) of their choice. As Brahman is present in everything, so he may be worshipped anywhere. Popular places of

Offerings made to Agni, the sacred fire, take the prayers of the worshippers to God

worship include the home, the temple, a river bank, the summit of a mountain, or at any other holy place. But there are no set rules about where or how Hindus should worship.

What part does the temple play in Hindu worship?

The temple is a sacred building which individuals or families may visit to perform personal acts of worship or puja. In Hinduism there is nothing which corresponds to daily or weekly congregational worship in the western sense – except in modern reform sects.

Temples are usually dedicated to a god or goddess. They are seen as the earthly home of the god, whose presence is shown by an image or statue in a shrine in the innermost part of the building. Worshippers visit the temple, making various offerings (upacharas), such as flowers and food to the god. They may pray or recite a sacred teaching, or chant known as a **mantra**. There is usually a priest in attendance at the temple who looks after the images and performs the daily rituals, reciting prayers from the holy scriptures.

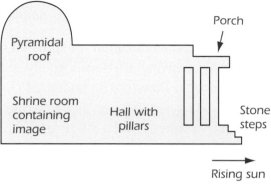

Pyramidal roof

Porch

Shrine room containing image

Hall with pillars

Stone steps

Rising sun

Swaminarayan Temple, Neasden, London

How do Hindus worship in the home?

Many Hindus set a corner of a room aside in their home as a shrine where the family can go to worship. The shrine usually contains a picture or statue of the family's favourite god or goddess. Family members will 'wake' the god there every morning with light, food and prayers. Food placed before the god is received back as prashad or 'blessed food'. The sacred name for Brahman (AUM or OM) may be chanted. The sacred prayer, Gayatri Mantra, is recited daily by most Hindus. In fact, the ceremonies that are likely to take place will be the same as the puja and arti ceremonies which take place in a temple.

What are the most important Hindu times?

Hindu festivals are sometimes seasonal, but also celebrate the myths of the scriptures and the life and activities of notable Hindus. Some festivals are celebrated across the whole of India, while others only take place in a small region. Three of the most important Hindus festivals for the whole of India are:

- **Divali** is the Hindu festival of light which takes place over five days in October/November and marks the Hindu New Year. Lakshmi, the goddess of good fortune and wealth is worshipped. New accounts books are opened by businesses, and everyone prays for good fortune in the New Year. The lights are to attract Lakshmi to one's house or business, and fireworks are let off to frighten away ill-fortune. Light symbolises the victory of goodness and virtue.

- **Holi** is a five-day festival where different myths tell of the defeat of a terrifying demon whose body was burned on a bonfire. There is often a great bonfire recalling this event. It is a relaxed and joyful occasion when past ill-feelings are forgotten and visits are made to friends.

- **Navaratri and Dassehra** Navaratri means nine nights. It is celebrated in honour of the goddess and there are nine nights of dancing to remember her defeat of the buffalo demon. Dassehra is the tenth day. The festival is a reminder of God's love and protection, of the belief that good will overcome evil, and that people should be loyal and caring to one another. It takes place in early autumn.

Divali

What holy places are special for Hindus?

For Hindus, making a pilgrimage to a holy site, of which there are many in India, is regarded as an important way of showing devotion to God and is thought to bring great blessings to those who make such a journey in the right spirit.

Holy places for Hindus are usually located on the banks of rivers, coasts, seashores and mountains. Because water is essential for life, Hindus believe that it comes from God and is a part of God. This is one of the reasons why rivers are often places of pilgrimage in India, in particular the River Ganges at Varanasi (Benares). Bathing is also important in Hinduism because it is believed that the worshipper must be in a state of cleanliness to appear before God to worship.

Pilgrims bathing in the River Ganges at Varanasi

While most Hindus hold that pilgrimage is a great honour, some question its worth, arguing that true pilgrimage is the inner journey of the soul.

Suchinderam temple and tank for ritual bathing in Tamil Nadu

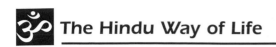

The Hindu Way of Life

How are class divisions viewed within Hinduism?

Traditionally, Indian society has been divided into four main religious groups (**varnas**):

- The priests (**Brahmins**), teachers and spiritual leaders.
- The nobles and warriors (**Kshatriyas**) who maintain law and good government.
- The merchants and peasants (**Vaishyas**) who are responsible for trade and commerce, agriculture and industry.
- The labourers (**Sudras**) who are craftsmen and manual workers.

What is the caste system?

As Indian communities grew and developed, the four main varnas became divided into a number of sub-classes (**jatis**) or caste groups. Caste is a social group into which a Hindu is born depending on the occupation or background of their parents. There are numerous castes, each with its own laws of purity, eating, marriage and social mixing. Caste defines a person's religious and social duties and responsibilities. Marriage and other social contacts have been traditionally kept within the same caste.

The three highest castes wear a sacred thread as a sign that they are twice born (see page 73, The student stage). A person remains within the caste into which they were born, but after they die they can be reborn into a higher or lower caste, or even as an animal, depending on whether or not they have lived a good life. Although the caste system ensured that all necessary tasks in society were performed, some aspects of it have been banned by the Indian government in recent times. This was because it did not allow people equality of opportunity and wasted much talent. Nevertheless, it is still very influential in villages, but less so in large towns and cities.

What is dharma?

Hindus believe that everyone has a duty in life. This duty or code of behaviour is called dharma. It also means righteousness, since to do your duty brings merit. There are duties which are shared by all Hindus. These are called Sadharan Dharma. Other duties are defined by caste.

Priests had a duty to ensure the spiritual well-being of the people. Rulers had a duty to ensure peace and stability. Those in business had to work hard to ensure that everyone was prosperous. Those who served were to do so honestly and without resentment. Finally, there were those duties which are defined by your stage of life. These were different for a student and a householder.

Today, most Hindus try to worship God in some form, do their duty to friends, family and society, work hard and tell the truth.

Cows wander freely. They are a sign of human dependence on Creation

What are the four stages of life?

All aspects of life for a Hindu are affected by their religion. They aim to show devotion to the divine in everything they do, from working in the fields or office to preparing food for a family meal. Many Hindus have a picture of a god or holy man with them at all times.

There are four stages of life according to Hindu teaching. These are called **ashrama** and they apply to the members of the three higher classes – the Brahmin, Kshatriyas and Vaishyas. Each stage is defined by a particular duty (dharma):

- **The student stage** – After childhood, the young person must take their education seriously and devote time to studying the sacred texts. This begins with the Sacred Thread ceremony. It marks a form of spiritual rebirth. The threads are symbolic of the debts owed to God, and the knot that ties them can represent knowledge of the Supreme Spirit. The thread should be worn throughout a person's life.

- **The householder stage** – Begins with marriage and involves rearing a family and serving the family and the community in accordance with Hindu principles.

- **The forest stage** – Corresponds to middle-age when the family have grown up and the person is free to spend time in reflection and meditation.

- **The ascetic stage** – Involves leaving the family and adopting the life of a recluse who separates himself from the rest of the world (sannyasin). The aim is

Circumambulating the sacred fire during the marriage ceremony

to live a life of meditation, in the quest for moksha. In this way it is seen as a preparation for death.

The final two stages are not often practised in modern times.

Saraswati: Goddess of learning and music. She is very popular with students

? Questions

1 Describe the origins of Hinduism.

2 Give an account of the main beliefs of Hindus.

3 Explain why many Hindus believe that it is impossible for a person to explain or understand Brahman.

4 What are the main sources of Hindu scripture?

5 Describe the ways in which Hindus might worship God.

6 Hindus seek to achieve eternal piece (moksha) through release from the cycle of death and rebirth. What do you think they mean by 'eternal peace'?

7 Hindus believe that they should do their duty to their family and friends. Give two examples of what this might mean.

5 Buddhism

 Buddhism: Essential Facts

Origins	India from the fifth century BCE
Present spread	Mainly Asia
Founders/Prophets	Siddattha Gotama (the Buddha)
Major beliefs	Release from pain and suffering through contemplation and a balanced way of life
Sacred writings	Tipitaka, The Suttas, The Shastras, The Tantras
Special places of worship	Temples, stupas, pagodas, natural features, and shrines in the home
Special times	Wesak, others are specific to regions
Religious teachers	Bhikkhus (monks), Bhikkhunis (nuns)
Places of pilgrimage	The Lumbini Grove, Bodh Gaya, Kusinara, Deer Park (Sarnath)
Holy day	No particular day of the week is special
Forms of worship	Meditation, good works
Groups	Theravada, Mahayana, Zen, Lamaism, Pure Land Buddhism

The Origins of Buddhism

What is Buddhism?

Buddhism is a religion that began in India about 2500 years ago. It grew and spread, and today there are more than 300 million Buddhists, mainly in Asia.

Buddhism is based on the teachings of the Buddha, a name which means 'Enlightened One'. The Buddha was born in India about 563 BCE, and died at the age of 80. He was originally called Siddattha Gotama.

Buddha rupa in a shrine in a temple

The Buddha realised that pain and suffering are part of our lives. But he believed that we can find release from suffering by understanding ourselves better. He said that much of our unhappiness comes from our greed and selfishness. So the Buddha worked out a way of life – the **Noble Eightfold Path** (see page 81) – which would help people stop their selfish desires. He called it the **Middle Way**. This means finding a thoughtful and balanced way to live and giving up greed and selfishness and not causing suffering to ourselves or others.

The Buddha did not believe in any god or gods or in a human soul. He said that we could not know if the universe is regulated by a spiritual force – a god or ultimate reality – which exists outside and above the laws of nature and the actions of human beings. Instead, he taught that in order to find happiness we must recognise that nothing is permanent or fixed and that we constantly have to work out for ourselves how to live a good and positive life.

The wheel is the symbol of Buddhist teaching. It has eight spokes which stand for the Noble Eightfold Path

What are the origins of Buddhism?

The founder of Buddhism Siddattha Gotama was a Hindu who travelled around India seeking enlightenment. Siddattha tried living as a Hindu holy man. He found that this caused him to suffer. When he became enlightened he took the name Buddha to describe his new found state.

Like all great gurus (teachers) Gotama attracted disciples who he formed into a band of monks (**bhikkhus**). He began to instruct them in the way of enlightenment. His teaching is known as the **Dhamma** and Buddhists must follow this if they wish to be freed from the cycle of rebirth. One of the teachings was that monks should live together in a community or brotherhood known as a Sangha. These groups of monks then became wandering preachers.

Bhikkhu (monk)

This is why Buddhists are now found all over southern Asia from India and Tibet to Thailand, Sri Lanka and Japan.

The original teachings were inevitably shaped by cultural differences and Buddhism is different in different countries. There are two main traditions of Buddhism in the world today:

- **Theravada** – The teachings of the elders, which are still practised today and are mainly monastic. This form is found in Thailand and Sri Lanka.

- **Mahayana** – In this form lay people play a greater part. It is possible for many to achieve enlightenment. It is mainly found in Japan, Bhutan, Nepal, Korea, Vietnam, Indonesia, etc. Tibetan Buddhists are followers of the Dalai Lama (lama means teacher). They were forced to leave Tibet and now live in northern India and other parts of the world. Vajrayana is another form where enlightenment comes like a vajra or thunderbolt. One form of this is Zen which originated in Japan.

Kelaniya Maha Vihara in Sri Lanka.
A stupa built where the Buddha taught

What do Buddhists believe about God?

Many Buddhists say that we cannot know if there is a God. For this reason some people do not think that Buddhism should be counted as a religion. Rather it should be seen as a way of life. Buddhists do, however, believe that their way of life will lead them eventually to a state called **Nibbana** (Nirvana) where they will escape from the suffering and illusion of this life.

Young Buddhists carrying their offerings

All Buddhists seek enlightenment. They believe that by self-discipline, contemplation and living according to the teachings of their leader they can achieve freedom from the cycle of rebirth (**Samsara**).

What are the central teachings of Buddhism?

Buddha realised that nothing in life is permanent. Everything changes – just think about how you have changed as you have grown up. This impermanence of things is called **anicca**.

Buddha had also seen that we all suffer in one way or another. He had seen sickness, old age and death. We all are subject to these and they make life unsatisfactory. This is called **dukkha**.

Finally, Buddha realised that everything is made of different parts. When we are gone these different parts are just reassembled to make something new. As a result of this he said that there is no such thing as 'I' or 'the self'. This is known as **anatta**, literally 'no atman'.

When Buddha realised these things he became enlightened. He described his enlightenment as Four Noble Truths:

1 **To exist is to suffer.** There is 'impermanence' (anicca) and all things come to an end.

2 **Suffering is caused by selfishness** and worrying about things that are not important.

3 **Suffering ceases once you deal with the cause.** Wisdom is achieved when a person understands the roots of their pain or misery.

4 **The Buddhist way of life** leads to the ending of suffering and the growth of wisdom.

Peace pagoda in Milton Keynes

What is the Buddhist way of life?

The Buddha went on to describe the Buddhist way of life as a 'Noble Eightfold Path'. The eight include:

- Right view
- Right thought
- Right speech
- Right behaviour
- Right livelihood
- Right effort
- Right awareness
- Right concentration.

What is meditation?

In many religions people try to understand the meaning of life by contemplating or thinking. Some people call this prayer. In many ways this is what is meant by meditation (**samadhi**). Buddhists adopt comfortable seating positions, or other body positions including walking, to help their contemplation. Any position which frees the mind and helps you to concentrate on ultimate questions would be acceptable.

Buddhists sharing the main meal at midday in a monastery. The food is provided by lay people who attend the ceremony

 **Buddhist Scriptures**

What are the main Buddhist scriptures?

The first Buddhist scriptures were written in Pali, the language of the Buddha. They are known as the **Tipitaka** which means three baskets. The three baskets are:

- The **Vinaya** which contains the rules for monastic living.
- The **Sutta** or teachings of the Buddha.
- The **Abhidhamma** which is a systematic attempt to explain the beliefs and ideas (philosophy) of Buddhists.

For many Buddhists the most important scriptures are found in the Sutta Pitaka. Here is where you find the **Dhammapada**, the way of teaching. All Buddhists accept this very important collection of sayings.

Another part of the Sutta Pitaka is the Jataka tales. These tell of the earlier lives of the Buddha. They give everyday examples of the sort of life a Buddhist should lead.

The Mahayana Buddhists accept the Tipitaka but also have a huge number of other sutras (threads) which offer further advice.

Buddhist Bhikkhu teaching

What are the duties of a bhikkhu?

All those belonging to a monastery must follow ten clear rules known as the **Das Sila**. These rules say that bhikkhus must avoid sexual misconduct and must **not**:

- kill
- steal
- tell lies
- use alcohol or drugs
- eat after midday
- take part in dancing or singing
- use garlands or cosmetics
- sleep in luxury
- accept money.

The first five of these rules should be followed by all Buddhists. In addition to this monks should meditate, read and study. They should perform any tasks which contribute to the community. Monks should also contribute to the whole community by providing teaching about Buddhism to lay Buddhists. The life of a monk is one of great joy in which they are allowed to concentrate on finding out more about the meaning of life and sharing it with the whole Buddhist community.

Young bhikkhus in Sri Lanka visiting the Temple of the Tooth in Kandy

✵ Buddhist Worship

How do Buddhists worship?

The emphasis on Buddhism is on an individual's liberation from samsara and his or her own need to achieve enlightenment in order for this to happen. Worship in Buddhism is, therefore, personal.

A Buddhist family worshipping at a shrine

In order to worship, Buddhists:

- visit temples and shrines
- offer fruit and flowers at the shrines or deities they visit
- chant mantras
- meditate
- walk clockwise around stupas
- burn incense or joss sticks
- prostrate themselves in front of a shrine
- use a prayer wheel
- bang cymbals when an offering is made
- sit in silence and listen!

What are the 'good works' of Buddhism?

Buddhism celebrates all that is good and pure. Buddhists are required to:

- follow the first five rules for monks
- support monasteries with gifts of food and robes
- give to the poor
- develop tranquillity and insight
- earn good **kamma** to try and break free from the cycle of samsara.

*Buddhists use beautiful gardens to produce tranquillity
and aid meditation*

Special Times and Pilgrimage

What are the Buddhist special times?

Buddhism does not focus greatly on special occasions. The majority of festivals that are celebrated are specific to particular countries, or even a small region within a country. There are no set ways of celebrating; what is more important is that the worshipper is following the example and teaching of the Buddha. There is, though, one festival that all Buddhists do celebrate. It is called **Wesak**:

- **Wesak** is celebrated in May or June at the time of the full moon. Buddhists remember the birth, enlightenment and death of the Buddha. As with other festivals, there may be processions and shrines in the home and temples may be specially decorated.

- **Rainy season retreat** – Many Buddhists still celebrate this time when in the past, because of the poor weather, Bhikkus could not travel and teach. They stayed in the monastery. Lay people made and still make offerings at this time, eg new robes. This is called Kathina. It takes place in the autumn.

- **Ceremonies** – There are no special Buddhist ceremonies for birth, marriage and death. In some Buddhist countries young boys may enter a monastery for a short time as part of their education. At this time a boy would adopt the life of a monk. He would only have a simple saffron robe, an alms bowl to receive offerings, a needle and thread, a razor, a string of beads and a strainer to remove insects from drinking water.

Elephants carry relics of the Buddha in special processions at important times

BUDDHISM

- **Pilgrimages** – Pilgrimage is not required in Buddhism, but many Buddhists like to follow in the footsteps of the Buddha. This can mean visiting four places:
  - Lumbini where the Buddha was born
  - Bodh Gaya where the Buddha was enlightened
  - The Deer Park where the Buddha gave his first sermon
  - Kushinari where the Buddha died.

There are also other important places which are usually associated with some event in the life of the Buddha, some leading Buddhist, or with a relic. Among these is Shri Maha **Bodhi** at Anuradhapura, Sri Lanka. Here, in a temple, stands a famous Bodhi tree. It was grown from a cutting taken from the tree under which the Buddha was enlightened. The original tree has since died and the trees at both Bodh Gaya and the Deer Park were both grown from cuttings taken from Shri Maha Bodhi. Shri Maha Bodhi is more than 2500 years old so visiting it offers a direct link to the Buddha.

Shri Maha Bodhi grown from a cutting of the tree under which Buddha was enlightened

? Questions

1 What is the origin of the name 'Buddhism'?
2 What are the four main beliefs that Buddhists share?
3 Explain the meaning of the term 'Bhikkhu'.
4 *'How can Buddhism be a religion when it does not have a God?'* How would you respond to someone who said this? Write your answer, giving reasons for what you have said.

6 Sikhism

 ## Sikhism: Essential Facts

Origins	North-west India in the fifteenth century CE
Present spread	Mainly in the Punjab, India, UK, USA and Canada
Founders/Prophets	Guru Nanak and his nine successors
Major beliefs	There is one God; all humans are equal; it is good to serve others; the need for community (Sadhsangat) support
Sacred writings	Guru Granth Sahib, Dasam Granth (the collected writings of Guru Gobind Singh)
Special places of worship	Gurdwara (Gateway to the Guru) and in the home
Special times	Gurpurbs (anniversaries of the birth or death of one of the Gurus), Vaisakhi, Divali, Hola Mohalla
Places of pilgrimage	Harimandir Sahib (The Golden Temple in Amritsar), the Five Takhts (Thrones of Spiritual Authority)
Holy day	No particular day of the week is special
Forms of worship	Prayers, listening to the Gurbani (the Teachings of the Guru) in the company of the Sat Sangat (True Believers), contemplation, etc

Origins of Sikhism?

What is Sikhism?

Sikhism is a religion that originated in the area of north-west India, known as the Punjab, at the end of the fifteenth century CE. It was founded by Guru Nanak (1469-1539 CE) whose inspired teaching appealed to a group of devoted followers.

Worldwide, there are about 15 million Sikhs. Most still live in the north Indian state of Punjab, but there are also many in other countries around the world.

Guru Nanak

What are the origins of Sikhism?

The founder of Sikhism, Guru Nanak, was a devout Hindu who travelled widely in India and elsewhere seeking truth. He even got as far as the Ka'bah in Makkah, the holy place of Muslims. He taught that God was everywhere, in all people and that there should be no fixed way of praying to Him.

Sikhs believe that Nanak was so holy he was born with a form of halo around his head. Nanak was concerned about the religious divisions in India. He was keen to establish beliefs which emphasised that religion:

- is open to all people
- sees all people as equal
- sees all people as brothers and sisters.

Like all great Gurus, Nanak attracted disciples whom he taught about his beliefs in God. His teaching is contained in the **Guru Granth Sahib** – the Holy Book of Sikhs – which also contains the teaching of the other **Gurus** who followed after him making Sikhism into the religion it is today.

The Guru Granth Sahib also contains the writings of Hindus and Muslims, among others.

Who were the other Gurus?

- **Guru Angad** (1504-52 CE) – Established the **Gurmukhi** script, the language of the Guru Granth Sahib.
- **Guru Amar Das** (1479-1574 CE) – He was well known for his social reforms. He banned the practice of 'sati' and condemned 'purdah' and the seclusion of women. He encouraged monogamy and the remarriage of widows.
- **Guru Ram Das** (1534-81 CE) – He founded the city of Amritsar. He excavated the tank or pool where the Golden Temple was later built. Amritsar means 'Pool of Nectar'.

Harimandir Sahib (The Golden Temple)

- **Guru Arjan** (1563-1606 CE) – Completed the tank at Amritsar and built a temple (Hari Mandir) at its centre. His greatest achievement was to collect together the writings of the Gurus and others into the 'Adi Granth' (First Collection). He was the first Guru to be martyred.

- **Guru Har Gobind** (1595-1644 CE) – Spent much time fighting persecution. He introduced the two swords representing 'Meeri' (worldly authority) and 'Peeri' (spiritual authority). He built the Baba Atal Tower, which stands near to the Golden Temple, in memory of his son, who died at the age of nine. Free food is still distributed from here regularly.

- **Guru Hari Rai** (1630-61 CE) – A strong, but extremely kind Guru; he distributed expensive medicines to those in need. He even helped the Emperor who had persecuted his father, Guru Har Gobind.

- **Guru Hari Krishan** (1656-64 CE) – The child Guru who died at the age of eight. He died from smallpox which he caught whilst visiting the capital, Delhi. A plague had broken out and he was blessing those who were suffering.

- **Guru Tegh Bahadur** (1621-75 CE) – Tried to live in peace and spread the teachings of the Gurus. He was persecuted and martyred for supporting Hindus who wished to worship in their own way.

- **Guru Gobind Singh** (1666-1708 CE) – The Saint-Soldier; he and the Sikhs were forced to defend themselves in battle. He established the **Khalsa** (the Community of Pure Ones). He also completed the writing of the Guru Granth Sahib. His own writings were later collected together in the Dasam Granth.

☬ Sikh Beliefs

What do Sikhs believe about God?

Sikhs believe that there is only one God and that He is without
form. They call their God '**Nam**' and believe that He is everywhere,
created everything, has no fear or hatred, was not born and does
not die. Sikhs regard God as close to each person and He is often,
therefore, called 'Father'.

What are the central teachings of Sikhism?

- **Monotheism** – Harimandir Sahib (The Golden Temple) has
  four sides, and on each side there is an entrance. This shows
  that people from all four corners of the Earth can come and
  worship there. Sikhs believe that all religions are ways to God.
  They believe in the unity of God which is remembered in their
  symbol the **Ik Onkar**, the **kara** (see page 93) and the unity of
  the Khalsa.

Ik Onkar – God is one

- **Reincarnation** – As with all religions that have come out of the
  Hindu tradition, there is a strong belief in reincarnation. Sikhs
  believe that the soul belongs to the Spiritual Universe which
  has its origins in God. For them, the purpose of life on Earth is
  to achieve the soul's reunification with God and this occurs if
  a person's behaviour stores up blessings – grace – from God.
  Consequently, a soul may need to live many lives before it is at
  one with God.

What are the five Ks?

Sikhism is a very visual religion. It uses symbols to communicate its beliefs. In **Punjabi**, the language of the Punjab region of India from which Nanak came, each of the symbols begins with the letter K:

- **Kesh** – Sikhs are taught that they must never cut their hair. This is called kesh. In order to keep it tidy most Sikh men will tie a knot in their hair and cover it with a turban (pagri). Those Sikhs and others who do not wear a turban will cover their head before going into the **Gurdwara** to pray.

- **Kangha** – To keep their hair in good condition, combing is very important. Sikhs carry a comb as a symbol of this. The comb is used to keep the hair tidy and clean.

- **Kirpan** – Sikhs carry a sword called a kirpan. They remind Sikhs of their duty to defend the weak and needy. Nowadays the kirpan is usually kept safely in a scabbard, except on ceremonial occasions.

- **Kachera** – Sikhs wear a large pair of shorts underneath their normal clothes. These were worn originally to allow maximum movement in battle but their use is purely religious today.

- **Kara** – All Sikhs wear a steel bangle as a symbol of the oneness of God. It is worn around the right wrist and is a replica of the circle in the **Khanda** (see page 94). The kara represents the eternal nature of God, which never comes to an end. It also reminds Sikhs that their hands have been given to do good works.

Sikhs worshipping in a Gurdwara

What other symbols are important to Sikhism?

- **Ik Onkar** – Around a Gurdwara and on the canopy over the **palki** you may see this distinctive Sikh symbol. It is a statement of faith that there is only one God and it comes from the **Mool Mantar**:

    'There is only one God
    Truth is his name
    He is the Creator
    He is without fear
    He is without hate
    He is timeless and without form
    He is beyond death, the enlightened one
    He can be known by the Guru's grace.'   (Guru Granth Sahib)

- **The Khanda** – The khanda is a double-edged sword that is used to stir the Amrit during the Amrit ceremony at which Sikhs become members of the Khalsa. It is also the name given to the symbol of Sikhism which is found on the Nishan Sahib (flag) which flies outside every Gurdwara. This symbol consists of two swords on the outside of a kara (circle) with a Khanda in the centre.

The Khanda which for Sikhs symbolises God's concern for truth and justice

What are the sacred Sikh scriptures?

The most important Sikh scripture is the Guru Granth Sahib. Sikhs do not question the contents of the Guru Granth Sahib; nor its meaning. Rather they treat it as a living Guru itself that contains truth, wisdom and guidance on how to live a good life. It was the tenth Guru, Guru Gobind Singh, who invested the Guru Granth Sahib with 'Guruship'. This meant that from then on only these sacred writings could be seen as having the same authority as a living Guru. From that time on the Guru Granth Sahib was treated as a real Guru.

Great ceremony is attached to the rising of the Guru Granth Sahib in the morning and its putting to bed at night. These ceremonies are carried out by the Granthi who fetches it from a separate room in the Gurdwara where there is a bed on which it can rest. During the day it lies on a palki (a beautiful canopy and throne like that used by an ancient emperor) that is usually decorated with very ornate images and flowers. The Guru Granth Sahib is covered by beautifully decorated cloths called Rumalas when it is not being read.

Worshippers come into the Gurdwara and show respect to the Guru Granth Sahib by lying stretched out on the floor in front of it. Great care is taken to protect the Guru Granth Sahib by its keeper, the Granthi. He or she also studies hard to learn how to explain its meaning during services.

Guru Granth Sahib being carried to bed at night

The Guru Granth Sahib is written in the form of a poem and nearly all of it is set to classical Indian tunes called **ragas**. Indeed its words are called hymns and are laid out in verses. They were originally written in a special language called Gurmukhi – meaning 'mouth of the guru' – which exists in no other place and comes from Punjabi, the spoken language of Nanak's homeland. Gurmukhi was specially developed to allow the different languages used in the Guru Granth Sahib to be written down. Verses from the Guru Granth Sahib are used at important times in a Sikh's life.

On what occasions is the Guru Granth Sahib read?

- **Akhand Path** – A non-stop reading undertaken by a team of readers over approximately a 48-hour period. This usually happens at festivals, important ceremonies or other special occasions.

- **Sadharan Path** – Reading of the Guru Granth Sahib usually completed over a period of one to two months.
- **Dusshera** – Ten-day reading to be completed after a person has died.

- At **Anand Karaj**, the marriage ceremony, the **Lavan**, the four marriage hymns written by Guru Ram Das are read. The couple then walk round the Guru Granth Sahib, keeping it on their right side, completing each round by bowing to the scriptures. This shows that they accept the vows they have taken.

Anand Karaj – The Ceremony of bliss; a Sikh wedding. The family is the basis of the community (Sadhsangat)

- **Diwan**, public worship; the main part of which is listening to the Gurbani, the teachings of the Gurus from the Guru Granth Sahib.
- Readings from the Guru Granth Sahib are made at random; this is called 'Hukam' which means according to the Will of God, meaning that God guides the selection that is chosen.

Sikh Way of Life

What is the Sikh way of life?

Nanak taught that the path to God was made possible by:

- worshipping and repeating the divine name of God
- keeping the company of the **Sat Sangat** (True Believers)
- living in the community of the Khalsa and caring for the needy by sharing the fruits of hard work
- performing **sewa**
- success in business or hard work (karo).

Sikhs would also say that the wearing of the five Ks is important.

Why are all Sikh men called Singh?

The name '**Singh**' means lion. It describes how members of the Khalsa should act. They should be both gentle and fearsome when faced with persecution or any other wrong. In this way Sikhs have gained great respect throughout the world. This name was given to Sikh men at the first **Vaisakhi** in 1699 CE by Guru Gobind Singh.

Why are all Sikh women called Kaur?

Guru Gobind Singh said that all Sikh women should adopt the name '**Kaur**', which means princess. It means that Sikh women should behave and be treated like princesses. This gave equal rights to women at a time when they had few rights. Many Sikh women have fought alongside men against persecution.

How do Sikhs worship?

The emphasis in Sikhism is on an individual's freedom from samsara and his or her own need to achieve enlightenment in order for this to happen. Worship in Sikhism is, therefore, a very personal thing except in major shrines of international importance. In order to worship, Sikhs:

- visit Gurdwaras (the Gateway or Doorway to the Guru – the name for the Sikh place of worship)
- offer fruit and flowers or money at the palki – the daily resting place of the Guru Granth Sahib
- the Guru Granth Sahib should be shown respect by the waving of the **chauri**
- listen to the Gurbani (the teachings of the Gurus) in the company of the Sat Sangat
- repeat and meditate on the name of God
- share sacred food – **karah parshad**
- share a communal meal in the **Langar** – communal kitchen and dining room.

While praying (Nam Japa) Sikhs will recite the **Japji** and other prayers at the appropriate time of the day. The **Rahit Maryada**, the Sikh code of discipline, also requires them to read sections of the Guru Granth Sahib in a specially laid out sequence. Sikhs may also use a set of 108 beads called a Mala. The phrase 'Waha Guru' – God is great – is chanted 108 times.

☬ Special Times

What are the Sikh special times?

- **Vaisakhi** – Commemorates the establishment in 1699 CE of the Khalsa under the direction of Guru Gobind Singh. The 300th anniversary was celebrated in 1999 CE by Sikhs all over the world. There was a huge gathering in Slough, Berkshire and a procession headed by the Guru Granth Sahib of about 20 000 people in Leicester.

300th anniversary Vaisakhi procession in Leicester

- **Gurpurbs** – Festivals celebrating important moments in the lives of the Gurus. Sometimes birth is being celebrated and at other times it is death or martyrdom. Not surprisingly the anniversary of Guru Nanak's birthday is celebrated with great enthusiasm. Gurpurbs are celebrated usually with an Akhand Path, and by concentrating on hymns written by that Guru and stories about their life.

- **Divali** – Celebrates the triumph of good over evil. It is characterised by the lighting of the Gurdwara with divas (lights). It recalls the release from prison of Guru Har Gobind along with the 52 Hindu princes he rescued. The divas were lit to welcome him home.

- **Hola Mohalla** – Is a time marked by rejoicing and festivity with meals, fairs and sports.

What other sacred ceremonies do Sikhs observe?

Amrit is the Sikh ceremony at which a man or woman becomes a member of the Khalsa. The person will be initiated using amrit (a mixture of sugar crystals and water that has been stirred with a double-edged sword). The mixture is drunk and sprinkled on the eyes and hair. During the ceremony those being initiated must recite the Mool Mantar and they are told the strict rules of the Khalsa that must govern their lives.

Sikhs celebrating Divali

What are the 'good works' of Sikhism?

Sikhs are required to:

- give alms to the poor and to support those in the community who are suffering
- protect the weak and needy
- abstain from alcohol, tobacco or other intoxicating substances
- make a good marriage with the support of older members of the family
- earn enough good karma (grace) to break the cycle of rebirth
- perform Sewa (service) either manual or intellectual work, or by giving things or money to help.

? Questions

1 What is the origin of the name 'Sikhism'?
2 What are the five Ks and what beliefs do they represent?
3 Explain the meaning of the term 'Langar'.
4 Identify and explain different ways in which Sikhs place the Guru Granth Sahib at the centre of their lives. How do you think this helps them to live their lives in a modern world?

7 Personal and Social Issues

The Family

How do different religions view the family?

All of the major world religions view the family as an important part of society. Most also teach that the family has a vital role to play in religious practice. Religious life may be focused on the home and the family in a number of ways:

- **Worship** – This may take place in the home on a regular basis and/or on special occasions such as ceremonies and festivals. Jews celebrate Shabbat with a special family meal and prayers in the home. Hindus and Buddhists may have a shrine in their home where they express their faith. Most religious people will have pictures or symbols in their home which help them focus on the key beliefs and practices of their faith.

- **Education** – The family provides the context in which children learn about their religion as the family practises its faith in the home. Family members of all ages may also study sacred texts at home and discuss their beliefs with each other.

- **Moral values** – Each person has duties and responsibilities within the family. They may also express love and concern for each other. In this respect the family is based on moral values and may be seen as an example of what all human relationships should be like. Children learn what is acceptable behaviour and the difference between right and wrong.

- **Community life** – The family is viewed as the cornerstone of the community in many religions.

Hindu mother and daughter celebrating Divali

What are the main beliefs about the family?

One widely held belief, in those religions which believe in God, is that the family is part of God's creation. Indeed, the divine is often described as a father figure and his human creations are seen as his family. Thus Christians refer to God as 'Our Father' and identify themselves as living within the 'Family of God'. They believe that people should live in family units because it reflects God's nature and intentions for humanity. Respect for parents, as in most religions, is one of the Commandments.

How is the importance of the family recognised?

There are many ceremonies and practices through which the importance of the family in religious life is recognised. These include the following:

- **Marriage** – This is regarded as the basis for family life and is usually marked by a special ceremony which may happen in the place of worship and/or include the use of sacred texts, prayers and practices.

- **Children** – They are regarded as very important. Special thanks are given for the birth of a child and there may be a ceremony to welcome the young person into the religious community or church. Most religions have special events for children, eg baptism, circumcision, naming.

- **Worship** – It is normal in most religions for family members to worship together on some or all religious occasions. The Christian Sunday Service, for example, is traditionally regarded as a family occasion and in some churches families are encouraged to come forward to take Holy Communion together. Ceremonies connected with Shabbat begin in Jewish homes. The Sikh family is regarded as the basis of the Sat Sangat (Community of True Believers).

- **Politics** – Religious organisations may seek to influence public debate on issues affecting the family. The Roman Catholic Church, for example, has opposed changes which make divorce easier to obtain and laws which make abortion freely available. Sikhs campaigned successfully about the law requiring the use of motorcycle helmets, as this would have affected the religious requirement to wear a turban.

What do the major religions teach about family roles?

A role is the behaviour that is expected of a person who occupies a particular status, such as a 'father' or a 'mother'. Most religions support the idea that family members have responsibilities towards each other, and that they should carry out their duties in a loving and caring way. For example, Christian family life is seen to be founded on:

- **Duty and responsibility** – Husbands and wives are to behave with due respect for each other; children are to respect their parents' authority; children are to be treasured and cared for; each individual should strive to maintain the harmony and stability of family life.

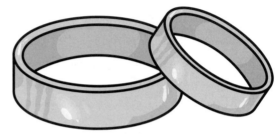

- **Love and care** – Family relations are based on a special kind of love and care that is both intimate and spontaneous. There is no burden or drudgery involved in carrying out the responsibilities of family life when it is a deeply held love that motivates the parent or child. Christianity teaches that the love and care which people give and receive within the family provides an example of how they should act towards others in the wider community.

What are the roles of husband and wife?

In religions that believe in God some interpretations of teaching suggest that through the act of creation God gave different qualities to men and women respectively.

It has been believed that men received qualities which made them good leaders and providers for their family, while women were to be better at expressing love and caring for people within the home. This particular teaching has been used to support the idea that the husband's role in the family is to be the breadwinner, while the role of the wife is to look after the house and care for the children and any elderly relatives (see Eph 4). Religious teaching has often been used to support cultural practices even when the teaching does not really support it!

However, not all religions or groups within particular religions accept that God created men and women differently, or that this can be used to justify the traditional division between male and female roles in the family. There is a greater willingness among many religions today to accept that it should be a matter of individual choice what roles husband and wife perform within the family, with the partners working out together an arrangement with which both are happy.

How should parents and children relate to each other?

Children have a special place in all of the major world religions. Life is seen as sacred and a young life is particularly valued. This may be because of the potential that a child has to enrich and strengthen the religious community. It may also be a way a giving thanks for the safe passage of mother and child through a dangerous stage of life – birth. The great religious teachers have encouraged parents to love and enjoy their children, to find

strength and increase their faith through them. Special care should be taken in rearing them so that they may have respect for and understand the requirements and teachings of the family faith.

Some religious sources also offer guidelines on how children should behave within the family. Christians and Jewish children, for example, are taught that it is important to respect your father and mother. Hindu law sets down clear rules for the student stage of life. In Islam there are strict guidelines about how parents and children should relate to each other.

Marriage

Is marriage sacred?

All the major faiths emphasise the importance of marriage and commitment between the parents of children. They view marriage as not only a civil or social contract, but also a spiritual union between the two parties that is full of religious significance. To say that marriage is sacred means that it expresses fundamental religious principles. Couples who share the same faith may confirm their commitment to these principles at a special wedding ceremony.

What is the Christian view of marriage?

Christianity teaches that marriage is monogamous (one partner only) and that it should be regarded as a serious lifelong commitment. Roman Catholics, Orthodox and many Anglicans view marriage as a sacrament (a sign of God's love or grace). The couple are spiritually joined together through the service.

Many Christian groups hold firmly to the Biblical teaching that sexual intercourse outside marriage is wrong. Sexual intercourse has the potential to create new life. The raising of a family needs the security and commitment of marriage. Adultery is wrong and in marriage the couple should foresake all others and bring honesty and loyalty to their union.

How is marriage viewed in other faiths?

Judaism teaches that marriage, called kidushin, is part of God's scheme for the world and for this reason it is important that a man should marry. Jewish law allows divorce, but marriage has always been regarded as a lifelong union, and with only one partner.

Generally, Jews view intermarriage (marrying someone from another faith) with sadness, although it is estimated that 30% of Jews marry outside the faith.

Hindu marriages are usually arranged between young people of similar status. Such marriages tend to be stable because they have the active support of both families to maintain the relationship. Also the experience of adults may result in a better choice of partner than the inexperience of the young.

Hindu wedding reception in Mumbai (Bombay)

Muslims believe that while marriage is a civil contract it is also a commitment to God and a dignified way of life, which is necessary for the creation of the next generation. It requires lifelong commitment to a partner(s), care and support for one's spouse and any children, stopping selfish desires and thinking about others, and rejecting sexual promiscuity. Most Muslim marriages are arranged, with the great emphasis being placed on the quality of the religious life of the bride and groom. According to Hadith (the traditions of the Prophet Muhammad) the girl in particular should have the opportunity to refuse the match. Sex outside marriage is not allowed, and is punishable according to the laws of Shari'ah.

How is marriage breakdown viewed by the major faiths?

The Christian Churches teach that marriage involves a pledge between husband and wife to remain together 'until death do us part'. However, views of divorce and remarriage differ between denominations. Officially, the Catholic Church does not allow divorce, nor does it remarry divorced people in church. Most other Christian Churches do allow divorce and may allow divorced people to remarry in church. They note that in one text Jesus taught that divorce can happen because of adultery. If one thing can break a marriage, then other things can do, too, but they have to be strong and serious reasons:

> *'I tell you that anyone who divorces his wife, except for marital unfaithfulness, and marries another woman, commits adultery.'*
>
> (Mt 19:9)

Divorce is permitted in Judaism, but it is customary for the husband to obtain an agreement from the 'religious court' (Beth Din). A wife or husband can refuse to be divorced in the Orthodox tradition, but in Israel a man can be imprisoned for refusing to divorce his wife. Religious Jews look upon divorce as a tragedy and with sadness.

A Jewish Ketubah – Marriage contract

Muslims believe that only if the marriage contract fails completely should it be broken, and then it should be terminated with honour and kindness. For example, theMdivorcing couple should respect each other's feelings and opinions, and discuss any differences in a civilised way. Normally after a divorce in Islam the father takes responsibility for the children.

For Hindus, marriage is expected to last for life. Much support is available for couples from the community of the extended family. It is similar for Sikhs, where marriage is regarded as the union of two families.

Why is the community an important part of religious life?

There is a communal aspect to all of the major religions. All suggest that in some way religious experience is made deeper and stronger through participating with others in a community of worshippers. This usually means more than simply attending the same services and festive occasions. Members of the community are encouraged to be open and warm towards each other, and to express their moral and religious beliefs in the way they come together as a community. As a community they may work together to serve others, especially the needy and less fortunate.

What binds the community together?

Shared beliefs and practices are important in bringing the faithful together and forming them into a community. Some religious communities are united by a common culture, too.

Jewish culture, for example, is based on a great body of customs and laws relating to matters such as food preparation, dress code, sexual relations, hygiene and education. Jews are also united by their identity as a nation and by the emphasis they give to Hebrew as their national language.

Sikhs have a distinctive way of life which emphasises the community and the struggle for a Sikh homeland known as Khalistan. The Langar (free kitchen) where food is served and shared by all, which is an important part of every Gurdwara, is one place where this is lived out in practice.

Sikhs performing sewa in the langar

In what ways might a person be involved in the life of the community?

Participating in public worship is the obvious way that people who share the same faith come together in a communal setting. Other shared experiences include:

- **Study** – Followers may study the sacred texts together. Christians have Bible study groups, for example, and Jews study the Torah and Hebrew at the synagogue. Muslim children will attend a Madrassah to learn Arabic at the end of the normal school day. Sikhs have Punjabi schools to ensure that their language and culture are maintained.

- **Ceremonies and special events** – These are often celebrated by the community together. Festivals, in particular, are seen as an occasion for the faithful to participate in communal activities.

- **Pilgrimage** – This may take a communal form as, for example, where a Christian congregation travel together to a place of pilgrimage, such as Lourdes and Walsingham. In Islam, the pilgrimage to Makkah is seen as a way of strengthening the individual's sense of identity with the Muslim community as a whole.

Christian pilgrimage to Walsingham

- **Community service** – Members of the same congregation may work together to serve others. Christians take part in a range of voluntary activities, for example, to help the needy and less fortunate. Sikhs are expected to perform sewa. Lay Buddhists should support bhikkhus with food and robes, and they are given teaching and other religious services in return.
- **Decision-making** – The public place of worship is sometimes also the location where the faithful come together to make decisions affecting the community. This is particularly the case in Judaism, Islam and Sikhism.

What do the major religions say about serving others?

Serving others is one of the highest values that the major faiths recognise. Rather than being concerned only about ourselves, our care and thoughts should be focused on other people, especially those who are unable to care for themselves. We may think about the family first when aiming to help others. But most religions teach that we should also consider what we can do to serve the wider community.

Helping those who are partially sighted

Almsgiving (Zakah) is important in Islam, for example, and Muslims who can afford it are encouraged to give part of their income to the poor. Sikhs are expected to perform sewa, by giving manual, intellectual or material service. Some Christians and Jews practise tithing by giving a proportion of their income to support religious causes. Many people from all religions are involved in charity work, raising funds for good causes and working with those less fortunate in the religious and wider community.

Freedom and Human Rights

What are human rights?

Human rights are rights which each
individual is said to have by virtue
of being a human person. They
are rights which are considered
necessary in order for a person to
live a fully human existence. Human
dignity is important in this respect.
A slave is a person whose dignity is
damaged because he is not free. The
right to freedom should, therefore, be
regarded as a basic human right. Other rights are the right to life, and
the right to adequate food and a basic standard of material comfort.

How are human rights viewed from a religious perspective?

All of the major religions teach that freedom and respect for life are
important values. In different ways they agree that each human life
has special meaning and that all should be free to seek salvation
through following their conscience and beliefs. No particular way
of life or pattern of thought should be forced on the individual.
Rather, the ideal from a religious perspective is that the main
influence on a person's behaviour and thoughts should be provided
by their religious faith.

Most religions accept that legal protection and rights may be
necessary in order to ensure that people are free to practise their
religion and to choose their own path through life. There are
differences of opinion, though, about what types of rights are
appropriate and how much individual freedom should be allowed.
Some countries where Islam is the main religion believe that
the Qur'an and other sacred writings should be consulted when
deciding what freedom and rights the individual should have
within the community. In other countries the civil law may be
given priority over religious law, though in western Europe much
civil law is based on Christian teaching.

Most of the major religions would make the following points:

- We are all part of Creation, and so to impose mistreatment on another person is an act against our own nature. Religions who believe in God would say that it is also an act against God, as God is the Creator.

- Freedom is necessary so that the individual may come closer to achieving the goals of their religious faith, and find their own way to salvation (though some religions teach that God's grace is also necessary in order to achieve salvation).

- Religious faith requires the believer to be humble, modest and adopt an attitude of service. Those who would abuse human rights value power and the ability to dominate other people, and this makes it difficult to find peace and spiritual truth.

- All religious beliefs should be tolerated and people should be free to follow their conscience in matters of faith.

In human affairs people should have the right to:

- a fair trial
- be treated as innocent until proven guilty
- equality of opportunity
- education
- a job
- association (forming together in a Trades Union or political grouping)
- freedom of movement
- free speech
- fair treatment in prison – no torture.

Every synagogue has a memorial to the millions killed in the Holocaust

What is the Christian response to the use of world resources?

Christianity teaches that God cares about the well-being of each person. No one should be left alone to suffer from hunger and poverty. The better-off have a duty to help the poor:

> *'The man with two tunics should share with him who has none, and the one who has food should do the same.'*　　　　(Lk 3:11)

Christians believe that God created the world for all to share and He created all humans as equals. The first priority in using the world's resources is to ensure that everyone's basic needs are met. No individual, group or country has the right to waste resources when there are other people who are starving or dying elsewhere in the world for want of necessary resources. Christians encourage people to work to achieve a fair distribution of resources. Christian organisations such as CAFOD (Catholic Fund for Overseas Development), Christian Aid and the Tear Fund work to relieve poverty in developing countries.

Indian shanty house

It is a Christian duty to care for the
Earth in the manner of a steward.
The Earth is entrusted by God to each
generation in turn. Each person has a
responsibility to look after the Earth
and its resources so that there is enough
for everyone and for future generations.

What do other religions teach?

Jews and Muslims also believe that resources should be used
carefully and fairly so as to minimise suffering and starvation in
the world. They emphasise God's compassion for the poor and His
desire that they should not be forgotten by people who are better
off. In Judaism charity is called zedakah (justice) and in theory, for
each Jew who can afford it, ten per cent of income is the correct
amount to give to charity. The best way for a Jew to help is to
use his money to help a poor person to become self-supporting.
Helping the poor and giving to charity is called Zakah in Islam and
it is an absolute duty.

Judaism teaches that God made the Earth and He made humans
to be in charge of the Earth. Jews have a religious obligation
to protect and guard God's creation. Islam also teaches that
humankind's role on Earth is that of trustee of God. Muslims
are required to participate in and support measures to conserve
resources and protect nature.

Hinduism in some respects has a different view of suffering.
It views problems such as poverty and starvation as part of
the natural order. Belief in reincarnation emphasises that any
suffering in this life is for a good purpose and will help us to be
better people in future lives. We will all have the opportunity to
experience both wealth and poverty.

Nevertheless, many Hindus are leading the way in projects to help the poor and to manage world resources more effectively. Hindus believe that God is part of his creation and can be approached through it. The cow is a symbol of our dependence on other animals and the whole of creation, so in the same way that Hindus protect and respect the cow they also believe in protecting the environment.

Hindu funeral pyre

? Questions

1 What qualities of God are like those of a father?

2 Write as a person who has strong religious beliefs explaining why you think family members ought to love and care for each other.

3 *'Why should I go out of my way to help other people?'* How might a person who has strong religious beliefs answer this question?

4 *'Everyone has the right to life.'* Write from a religious perspective justifying this statement.

5 Explain what the major religions teach about the way world resources should be used.

Glossary

✝ Christianity

AD	Anno Domini. In the Year of our Lord.
Advent	Period of religious observance beginning on the fourth Sunday before Christmas.
Altar	Table used for Eucharist.
Anglican	A person who is a member of the Church of England and recognises the leadership of the Archbishop of Canterbury.
Apocrypha	Books of the Old Testament that are in the Greek but not in the Hebrew Canon.
Apostle	Messenger who preached the gospel of Jesus, particularly the 12 disciples.
Ascension	The event, 40 days after the Resurrection, when Jesus 'ascended into heaven'.
Ash Wednesday	The first day of Lent.
Baptism	Rite of initiation into the Church involving immersion in, or sprinkling with, water.
BC	Before Christ. Period of history.
Confession	One of seven sacraments observed by some Churches whose priest hears a person's admission of wrong-doing confidentially.
Confirmation	The sacrament given to a baptised Christian at an age when they can understand its meaning.
Creed	Summary statement of religious beliefs, often recited in worship.
Easter	Central Christian festival which celebrates the resurrection of Jesus from the dead.
Ecumenism	Movement within the Church towards cooperation between the denominations and eventual unity.
Eucharist	A special thanksgiving service which focuses attention on the sacrificial death and resurrection of Jesus Christ.
Free Churches	Denominations which reject any link between Church and state; also called non-conformists.
Good Friday	The Friday in Holy Week. Commemorates the day Jesus died on the cross.
Gospel	The early accounts of Jesus' life and works.
Grace	Blessing. The freely given and unmerited favour of God's love for humanity. Also a prayer of thanks before or after meals.

Holy Communion	See **Eucharist**.
Holy Spirit	The third person of the Holy Trinity.
Holy Week	The week before Easter, when Christians recall the last week of Jesus' life on Earth.
Incarnation	The idea that God took human form in Jesus Christ.
Lent	The 40 days leading up to Easter.
Liturgy	Divine service according to a set ritual, such as Evensong or Eucharist.
Lord's Supper	See **Eucharist**.
Mass	Term for the Eucharist used primarily by the Roman Catholic Church.
Messiah	Saviour. Another name for Jesus Christ.
New Testament	Collection of 27 books forming the second section of the Bible.
Non-conformist	Protestant Christian bodies which became separated from the Church of England in the seventeenth century.
Old Testament	That part of the Bible which the Christian Church shares with Judaism, comprising 39 books.
Orthodox	The Eastern Orthodox Church.
Penance	Doing something to show sorrow for sin.
Pentecost	The day when the Holy Spirit appeared to the early Christians.
Pope	The Bishop of Rome, the head of the Roman Catholic Church.
Protestant	Major division of the Christian Church, distinct from Roman Catholic and Orthodox churches.
Psalm	A poem or hymn in the Old Testament.
Resurrection	The rising from the dead of Jesus Christ.
Roman Catholic	Christians who recognise the authority of the Pope in Rome.
Sacrament	A religious ceremony regarded as the outward sign of spiritual blessing.
Saint	A person whose Christian life is an example to others.
Salvation	Uniting people with God, which brings new life and peace.
Sin	An act of disobedience against the known will of God.
Supplication	Praying for help.
Trinity	Three persons in one God; the Father, the Son, and the Holy Spirit.

☪ Islam

Adhan	Call to prayer made five times a day.
al-Madinah	Medina.
Allah	The Islamic name for God.
Arafat	A plain near Makkah where pilgrims gather to worship, pray and ask for forgiveness.
Eid-ul-Adha	Festival of Sacrifice.

Eid-ul-Fitr	Festival to mark the end of Ramadan.
Fard	Obligatory duty according to divine law.
Fatwa	A legal opinion according to Islamic teaching.
Hadith	The sayings and deeds of the Prophet Muhammad.
Hafiz	Someone who has learnt the Qur'an by heart.
Hajj	Annual pilgrimage to Makkah.
Halal	Anything which is permitted or lawful in Islam.
Haram	Anything unlawful or not permitted.
Hijrah	The journey of the Prophet Muhammad from Makkah to Madinah in 622 CE.
Iblis	The Jinn who defied Allah by refusing to bow to Adam and later became the tempter of all human beings.
Ibrahim	Abraham.
Ihram	White garments worn by pilgrims on the Hajj.
Imam	A person who leads the communal prayer.
Iqamah	Call to stand up for Salah.
Islam	Peace attained through willing obedience to Allah's divine guidance.
Jihad	Personal struggle against evil.
Ka'bah	Sacred cube-shaped building in Makkah.
Makkah	Mecca.
Masjid	Mosque – Muslim place of worship.
Mihrab	Niche or alcove in mosque wall indicating the direction of Makkah.
Minbar	Pulpit.
Mu'adhin	Caller to prayer. Known in English as 'muezzin'.
Muhammad	Name of the final Prophet.
Muslim	A person who has accepted Islam.
Pillars of Islam	The five basic requirements for being a Muslim.
Qur'an	Sacred book of Islam. The book revealed to the Prophet Muhammad by the Angel Jibril.
Rak'ah	Cycle of movements and words used at prayer.
Ramadan	The month of fasting.
Sadaqah	Voluntary payment or good action for charitable purposes.
Salah	The five daily prayers.
Sawm	Fasting from just before dawn until sunset.
Shahadah	The Islamic declaration of faith.
Shari'ah	Islamic law based upon the Qur'an and Sunnah.
Shi'ite	A Muslim sect which believes in the succession of Ali.
Sujdah	Prostration.
Sunnah	Model practices, customs and traditions of the Prophet Muhammad.
Sunni	Muslims who believe in the succession of Abu Bakr.

Surah	Chapter of the Qur'an.
Tawaf	Walking seven times around the Ka'bah in worship of Allah.
Tawhid	Belief in the unity of Allah.
Ummah	The Islamic community.
Wudu	Ritual washing or ablution before Salah.
Zakah	Welfare payment as an act of worship.

 Judaism

Agadah	Telling. Rabbinical teachings on moral values.
Aron Hakodesh	Holy Ark. The focal point of the synagogue, containing Torah scrolls.
Bar Mitzvah	Ceremony of initiation for a 13-year-old boy.
Bat Mitzvah	Ceremony of initiation for a 12-year-old girl, recognised in some progressive Jewish sects.
Bet ha Knesset	House of Assembly. Synagogue.
Brit Milah	Circumcision.
Circumcision	Religious rite of Brit Malah, performed by a qualified Mohel on all Jewish boys, usually on the eighth day after birth.
Gemara	Commentary on how to interpret the Mishnah.
Halakhah	The way. The code of conduct encompassing all aspects of Jewish life.
Hannukkah	An eight-day festival of lights to celebrate the rededication of the temple following the Maccabean victory over the Greeks.
Hebrew	Ancient language used by Jews for prayer and study; also everyday language in Israel today.
Kabbalah	Jewish mysticism.
Kaddish	Prayer publicly recited by mourners.
Ketuvim	Third section of the Tenakh.
Kippah	Skull cap worn during prayers and Torah study, etc.
Kosher	Jewish dietary laws.
Mezuzah	Scroll placed on doorposts of Jewish homes, holding small sections of the Torah, often in decorative case.
Midrash	Commentary and interpretation of the Tenakh.
Mishnah	Oral teachings providing guidance on Jewish laws.
Nevi'im	Second section of the Tenakh.
Noachide Laws	Seven laws given to Noah after the flood, which are incumbent on all humankind.
Pesach	Festival commemorating the Exodus from Egypt.
Pikei Avot	Sayings of the Fathers. Part of the Mishnah.
Purim	Festival commemorating the rescue of Persian Jews as told in the book of Esther.
Rabbi	Ordained Jewish teacher.

Rosh Hashanah	Jewish New Year.
Seder	Pesach (Passover) meal.
Shabbat	Hebrew name for the Sabbath, the weekly day of holy rest.
Shavuot	Feast of Weeks. One of three pilgrim festivals celebrated in summer, seven weeks after Pesach.
Shema	Major Jewish prayer proclaiming the unity of God.
Sukkot	Feast of Tabernacles. One of three Biblical pilgrim festivals, it is celebrated in the autumn.
Synagogue	Meeting place for Jewish life and worship.
Tallit	Prayer shawl.
Talmud	Book containing details and discussion of oral law.
Tefillin	Small leather boxes containing passages from the Torah.
Tenakh	The Jewish Bible comprising Torah, Nevi'im and Ketuvim.
Torah	The first five books of the Jewish Bible.
Yom Kippur	Autumn festival of atonement.

ॐ Hinduism

Arti	Welcoming ceremony in which light is circled before the deity or saintly people to show respect.
Ashrama	Stage of life.
Atman	The real self or soul of each person.
Avatar	Descent or incarnation of the god Vishnu who comes to save the Earth from a terrible evil.
Bhagavad Gita	Popular Hindu scripture of the Bhakti tradition, featuring Krishna as the charioteer of Arjuna.
Bhakti	Devotion.
Brahma	Hindu god – the creator.
Brahman	The supreme spirit or god whom Hindus worship in different forms.
Brahmin	The main social grouping from which priests are drawn.
Dassehra	Festival celebrating the victory of Lord Rama over Ravana.
Dharma	Religious duty.
Divali	Festival of lights at the end of one Hindu year and beginning of the new year.
Guru	Spiritual teacher.
Havan	Act of worship in which offerings are made into the sacred fire.
Holi	Festival of colours, celebrated in Spring.
Jati	Occupational grouping.
Jnana	Knowledge.
Karma	Action and the results of action. Also refers to the law of cause and effect.

Mahabharata	Hindu epic poem.
Mandir	Temple.
Mantra	Short sacred text or prayer, often chanted repetitiously.
Marg	Path.
Maya	Illusion.
Moksha	Ultimate liberation from the cycle of birth and death.
Navaratri	The Nine Nights Festival preceding Dassehra.
Puja	Worship in the home or temple in the form of offerings to an honoured guest or a monarch.
Ramayana	Epic story of Rama and Sita.
Rishi	A spiritually wise person.
Samsara	The cycle of birth and death.
Sanatan Dharma	The eternal or imperishable religion.
Sanskrit	Sacred language of the Hindu scriptures.
Shaivites	Followers of Shiva.
Shaktas	Followers of the goddess.
Shakti	Energy or power. The followers of the many forms of the goddess.
Shiva	Hindu god – the destroyer and creator.
Shruti	Hindu scriptures said to be based on 'that which is heard'.
Smriti	Hindu scriptures said to be based on 'that which is remembered'.
Upanishad	Sacred writings based on the teachings of a guru.
Vaishnaites	Followers of Vishnu.
Varna	The four principle divisions of the Hindu caste system.
Veda	Any of the four Vedas, which are Hindu sacred writings.
Vishnu	Hindu god – the protector.
Yoga	A physical and spiritual discipline intended to help a person make contact with their soul.

⊛ Buddhism

Abhidhamma	Part of Tipitaka. Further or higher teaching.
Anatta	There is no individual self.
Anicca	The impermanence of things.
Bhikkhu	A disciple or monk within Buddhism.
Bodhi	Tree under which the Buddha realised enlightenment.
Dhamma	The teachings of the Buddha.
Dhammapada	The teachings of the Buddha in written form.
Dukkha	Suffering; ill; unsatisfactoriness; imperfection.
Kamma	The goodness that people store up in order to be liberated from the cycle of samsara.
Mahayana	The northern tradition of Buddhism.

Nibbana	The place that Buddhists seek to attain by building up Kamma.
Samsara	The cycle of birth, death and rebirth.
Sutta	Part of Tipitaka. Written sections of Buddhist teaching.
Theravada	The southern tradition of Buddhism.
Tipitaka	Three baskets. Three texts – Vinaya, Sutta and Abhidamma.
Vinaya	Part of Tipitaka. Rules for living in Buddhist community.
Wesak	Festival recalling the birth, enlightenment and death of Buddha.
Zen	The Japanese and far eastern traditions of Buddhism.

Sikhism

Akhand Path	Continuous reading of the Guru Granth Sahib from beginning to end.
Chauri	Symbol of the authority of the Guru Granth Sahib. Fan waved over scriptures, made of yak hairs or nylon.
Divali	The Sikh festival of light.
Diwan	Worship.
Dusshera	Ten-day reading of the Guru Granth Sahib when a person dies.
Gurdwara	Sikh place of worship.
Gurmuhki	The language in which the Guru Granth Sahib is written.
Gurpurbs	Commemorative days of the Gurus.
Guru	Teacher. Refers specifically to the first ten teachers who helped to establish Sikhism as an independent religion.
Guru Granth Sahib	The holy book of the Sikhs.
Hola Mohalla	The Sikh version of the Hindu festival of Holi.
Ik Onkar	The symbol of Sikhism which refers to the oneness of God.
Japji sahib	A morning prayer.
Kachera	Traditional shorts/underwear. One of the five Ks.
Kangha	Comb worn in the hair. One of the five Ks.
Kara	Steel bangle worn on the right wrist. One of the five Ks.
Karah parshad	Sacred food distributed by worshippers in the Gurdwara.
Kaur	Princess – Name given to all Sikh females by Guru Gobind Singh.
Kesh	Uncut hair. One of the five Ks.
Khalsa	The Sikh community.
Khanda	Double-edged sword.
Kirpan	Sword. One of the five Ks.
Langar	Communal kitchen in which Sikhs share a meal.
Lavan	Sacred wedding vows said before the Granth by a couple committing to marriage.
Mool Mantar	Basic teaching. A chanted prayer of Sikh worshippers.
Nam	The Sikh name for God.
Palki	Resting place for the Guru Granth Sahib during the day.

Punjabi	The original spoken language of the region of Guru Nanak's origins.
Raga	Classical Indian tune.
Rahit Maryada	Sikh code of discipline.
Sat Sangat	Community of True Believers.
Saht Sangat	Community of Pure Believers.
Sewa	Charity in the name of all humanity.
Singh	Lion – Name taken by all Sikh males.
Vaisakhi	The festival which celebrates the formation of the Khalsa.

Abbreviations

Acts	Acts of the Apostles
AD	Anno Domini in the year of our Lord (Christian Calendar)
BC	Before Christ
BCE	Before Common Era
CE	Common Era
Dt	Deuteronomy
Eph	Ephesians
Ex	Exodus
Gn	Genesis
1 Cor	St Paul's First Letter to the Corinthians
Jn	John
Lk	Luke
Mk	Mark
Mt	Matthew